I0825502

PRAISE FOR

BECOMING THE WARRIOR

"Meeting your goals takes clarity of mind, vision, and most importantly, a foundation of confidence. Jenn Donahue's Warrior Framework will show you how to combat thoughts before they undermine your work, so you can build an unshakeable foundation."

—JOSH LINKNER, FIVE-TIME TECH ENTREPRENEUR, *NEW YORK TIMES* BESTSELLING AUTHOR, AND VENTURE CAPITALIST

"If you have wanted a road map to help you achieve more and lead with clarity and confidence, this book lays it all out there for you! Jenn provides the framework to help you silence self-doubt, act with intention, and find the warrior inside."

—ALISON LEVINE, *NEW YORK TIMES* BESTSELLING AUTHOR OF *ON THE EDGE*; FACULTY, THAYER LEADERSHIP AT WEST POINT

"Jenn Donahue is the real deal. With compassion, she hands you the playbook for leading with strength and authenticity, and you will feel ready to step up, stand out, and become a warrior. A must-read!"

—ALDEN MILLS, FORMER US NAVY SEAL PLATOON COMMANDER, INC. 500 CEO, AND BESTSELLING AUTHOR OF *BE UNSTOPPABLE*

"Having served with Jenn Donahue in the US Navy Seabees, witnessing her as one of the most effective commanding officers I've known, *Becoming the Warrior* clearly reflects her exceptional leadership and profound understanding of human emotions and interpersonal dynamics. This book is a powerful, practical guide that offers tools to silence your inner critic and build unwavering confidence—a quality I saw her inspire in countless service members. Essential for anyone facing self-doubt or fear, it empowers you to take courageous, intentional action even in the face of uncertainty, unleashing your full potential. A must-read for leaders at every level!"

—REAR ADMIRAL MARK HANDLEY, CEC, USN (RETIRED), FORMER COMMANDER OF THE FIRST NAVAL CONSTRUCTION DIVISION

"*Becoming the Warrior* strikes the perfect balance of validating, empowering, and actionable. Jenn doesn't just offer perspective on self-doubt; she provides a clear path to overcome it. This isn't about blind confidence; it's about building the kind of self-trust that can weather fear, doubt, and setbacks. Whether you're leading others or just trying to show up fully for yourself, this book helps you fight the right battles—and win."

—MICHELLE "MACE" CURRAN, COMBAT VETERAN, FORMER USAF THUNDERBIRD PILOT, AND AUTHOR OF *THE FLIPSIDE*

"Exceptional book—deeply compelling stories plus a methodology that will actually make a difference in your life. For all who have ever felt they were not good enough or smart enough, or needed to prove themselves over and over . . . run, don't walk, to get a copy, and follow the advice. You won't regret it."

—WANDA T. WALLACE, PHD, MANAGING PARTNER AND FOUNDER, LEADERSHIP FORUM; AUTHOR, *YOU CAN'T KNOW IT ALL*; PODCAST HOST, *OUT OF THE COMFORT ZONE*; COACH; AND SPEAKER

"This book cuts through the noise with clarity and conviction. Jenn offers not just insight, but transformation—guiding readers with truth, courage, and a clear path forward. With sharp observation and unflinching honesty, she navigates the inner terrain of leadership—where fear, self-doubt, and the inner critic too often dominate. This book is not just inspiring; it is practical, wise, and urgently needed. For anyone who's ever felt overwhelmed by the demands of leadership or unsure of their own voice, Jenn is the trusted guide you've been waiting for."

—SHANNON HUFFMAN POLSON, AUTHOR OF *THE GRIT FACTOR* AND FOUNDER OF THE GRIT INSTITUTE

"The tools inside this book can help anyone get out of their own heads, lean into their strength and skills, and overcome imposter syndrome long enough to do the work they are meant to do."

—PHIL GERBYSHAK, US NAVY VETERAN, AUTHOR, AND PODCASTER

"Confidence is a key part of communicating ourselves to others, and Jenn Donahue's *Becoming the Warrior* will have you communicating your best self. She's brought together research, experience, and her personal struggle to build a framework for confidence that will hold you up through the hard times and support your success."

—DORIE CLARK, AUTHOR OF *THE LONG GAME* AND *REINVENTING YOU*

"Anyone working hard to achieve their dreams will one day ask themselves, 'Do I deserve this?' Jenn Donahue's new book gives you the tools you need to answer with a resounding 'Yes!'"

—JACQUELYN LANE, PRESIDENT AND CO-FOUNDER OF 100 COACHES AGENCY, *WALL STREET JOURNAL* BESTSELLING AUTHOR

JENN DONAHUE

BECOMING THE WARRIOR

HARNESSING *Your* INNER STRENGTH *to* SILENCE SELF-DOUBT

amplify
an imprint of Amplify Publishing Group

www.amplifypublishinggroup.com

Becoming the Warrior: Harnessing Your Inner Strength to Silence Self-Doubt

For more information, please contact:
Amplify Publishing, an imprint of Amplify Publishing Group
620 Herndon Parkway, Suite 220
Herndon, VA 20170
info@amplifypublishing.com

Library of Congress Control Number: 2025909903

CPSIA Code: PRV0825A

ISBN-13: 979-8-89138-645-7

Printed in the United States

To my loving husband, Sean, my supportive mom, my office manager, Pliny, and the two knucklehead interns: Fenris and Freya. You all made this possible.

But also to you, dear reader, may you find your inner strength within these pages.

CONTENTS

INTRODUCTION

"I'm just too busy."

Lynn had told herself that for years. She had a good job, a spouse, and two kids. They lived a comfortable lifestyle. Trips to either hockey or swim practices dominated weekends.

But her dream lay on a different path than the one she was on.

In her heart, she wasn't satisfied with her current job as a financial analyst and knew she could be much more. She wanted to go back to school and study law. Going to night school seemed daunting. Quitting her job and living on only one income was harrowing. Finding the time to take classes and study appeared insurmountable. Plus, she would talk herself out of it, thinking she probably wasn't smart enough anyway. It was just easier to say, "I just don't have time."

Before reading my book, she told me, "It feels like a piece of my life is missing. I'm not fulfilled. I want an opportunity to make a positive impact on the world, feel challenged, and have a sense of pride in what I do. But I don't think it's the right time."

In contrast, I have been confident, even a little cocky, for most of my life. I saw a challenge, and my first instinct was to run full speed ahead, relishing the idea of smashing through whatever stood in my way. But I fell hard—really hard—during one of these challenging times and had to figure out how to pull myself back up. Besides the realization that I wasn't infallible, I let the concepts of self-doubt, lack of confidence, and impostor syndrome take residence in my mind. And when you're a confident person who falls, sometimes you fall harder.

Anytime a new challenge would come up, that confident/cocky self I had once known was gone. I would turn inward and begin hearing little voices tell me, *I'm not good enough. I'm not worthy. I'm not ready.*

Whether you relate to Lynn in that you have a seemingly impossible goal but have done a good job of talking yourself out of it, or like me, you let a lack of confidence, the impostor syndrome, or self-doubt inhibit moving forward, this book is for you.

When I started writing this book, I had a mission. A few years ago, I created the Warrior Framework. It helped me to find a better version of myself. When talking with many others, I realized how they struggled with the same issues and the Warrior Framework could work for them. Convinced of this idea, my purpose was clear: I knew I could also teach it to you because it can work for you too.

As an engineer, I want to find the science behind what is going on in my brain. I am naturally wired to deconstruct ideas, and even my feelings, to get to the root of the matter. After a few months of mean little voices and inner critics holding sway over my decisions, I wasn't satisfied with telling myself, "Oh well, maybe I'll get better," because I wasn't getting any better. It felt like a great, open-ended problem that needed to be solved.

And as a combat veteran, I couldn't allow what seemed like a new enemy to invade my consciousness. I needed a resolution, and I needed proof that this resolution would work. In the military, I served in a section of the US Navy that built entire bases in the middle of deserts crisscrossed by insurgents and the occasional tumbleweed. We had to be sure that we could get in, get things built, repack, and do it again somewhere else on very prescribed timelines. We needed the right people, gear, and materials to make sure everything worked because hot on our heels were the US Marines, ready to take over the base and run operations.

There was no "Maybe this will work" or "Let's hope this works." There were no mulligans, no do-overs. Every part of the mission had to align, like the gears in a clock. This type of work requires research, detailed planning, and a strong will to keep everything and everyone organized and, most important, alive. It's like trying to herd cats into a shower.

I brought that same energy to trying to solve my internal problems. I needed proof, evidence, and results. I had to be able to get back up and do so quickly because there were things I wanted to do. And you have things you want to do.

The truth is that all of us seem to have a couple of voices in our head. One of them spouts mean little sayings like *You aren't good enough*. The other is wonderful at having us dillydally instead of taking on the hard tasks that will lead us further down the right path.

We often choose to listen to the excuses and lies that these voices tell us. Why? They may sound like our basic instincts that are designed to keep us safe. So we trust them without question. Yet these same voices are the ones that zap our confidence, allow impostor syndrome to fester, and create fear.

You see, we have been looking at impostor syndrome, self-doubt, and the fear of failure or success the wrong way. Many books help you to deal with these feelings once they have taken hold. But what if you got in front of these emotions before they started to entrench and manipulate your decision process? What if you are so prepared to tamp them down that they become quieter and less frequent? What could you accomplish? And that's only the beginning of what you are about to learn in this book.

Throughout this book, I ask you to complete a series of exercises. Some will be easy; some will force you to look deeper into what's going on in your head.

It may get a little uncomfortable, but only by understanding the root of where the voices come from can you learn to manage them.

I encourage you to have a notebook and sticky notes to start with. As we get into the book, one of the best ways of learning and retaining information is to write things down.

Each exercise is backed by science and social proof. I give you every fighting chance you need to help you achieve that most ambitious goal or that most outrageous dream.

Take. Your. Time. You might be tempted to power through some sections, but give yourself time to read each word. This is not a book to rush through. Allow yourself to take it all in. If you make the effort to work through each exercise, you're more likely to achieve astonishing results. Lynn, whom you met earlier, is realizing her dream. She took her LSATs and enrolled in a flexible evening program at Georgetown University to accommodate her schedule. Others who read my book have called or written me to say that they have newfound confidence or found a radical means to recognize and shut down their inner critics before they can cause harm. They did the work, and it paid off.

It may get a little uncomfortable, but only by understanding the root of where the voices come from can you learn to manage them.

Here's my promise to

you. By the end of this book, you will have the tools not only to recognize your inner critics but also to use a counterpoint to shut them down and move forward with confidence.

Are you ready?

Let's do this!

1

NEXUS EVENTS

He was the one. At sixteen years old, I knew that Russell encompassed everything that I could ever want in a boyfriend. We started dating as sophomores and were inseparable. We did our homework together; we rode our bikes around town. Even our parents got along well. Between the summer of our junior and senior years, Russell started to lift weights. Since we saw each other every day, I didn't notice the gradual changes. His baby fat started to drop off, and muscle started to grow. When we went back to school, I was dating the hottest guy in the band.

Our senior year was magical. We had most of our classes together, so we spent the evenings working on homework. We took our SATs, sent in our college applications, went on spring break, and started to gear up for graduation and prom, although in West Texas, we didn't call it prom. Our high school had an ancient tradition of the CATOICO (cattle, oil, and cotton) dance. Like any other seventeen-year-old girl, I was over the moon to go to CATOICO with Russell, who was inching his way up the ranks to become one of the hottest guys in the entire school. But more importantly, he was my best friend.

I chatted with my girlfriends about what dress I would wear

and whether we should go to Chili's or Outback Steakhouse before CATOICO. In other words, we spent much of our time planning the entire evening.

Then in early April, Russell wanted to talk. I was kind of excited about this. What could we talk about? He had already given me his class ring. Did he want to take our relationship up a notch? We were both going to Texas A&M in the fall, but it seemed a little too early to start talking about engagements. I remember sitting on the couch in his living room, filled with anticipation.

He wanted to date other people. He thought it was wise to see who else might be out there. If it was meant to be, we would find each other again. He broke up with me.

I didn't see it coming.

I was devastated.

I lost my best friend. I lost my homework partner. I lost one of the hottest guys in school. I probably would not be going to CATOICO.

I moped around all week, just going through the motions. Then the news broke.

Russell was going to CATOICO with Angela.

Angela!

Angela was also in the band, and we had several classes together.

My universe shattered, I drove home from school, ran up the stairs to the apartment I shared with my mom, darted to my room, slammed the door, and hurled myself on the bed. I curled up in the fetal position and sobbed. Not the cute sobbing. No, it was the real ugly cry where everything hurts. I was inconsolable.

What if he had broken up with me just to date Angela?
What if the last two years had all been a lie?
What if he never really loved me after all?

What if I was undatable?
What if . . .
What if . . .
What if . . .

The what-ifs raged inside my head, one after another, until I was completely consumed by my thoughts. I might have been hungry or tired, but there was no room for thoughts like these. All I knew was the cocoon of misery I created.

At some point, my mom came home and stood in the doorway, arms crossed. I wailed my what-ifs at my mother. As I said, it was just my mother and me. She had recently gone through a divorce and had to provide for both of us. My mom, so much stronger than I realized, exasperatedly said, "That's enough! You are making this all up in your head." But she didn't stop there. She then said something incredibly profound: "Are you going to let your head win?"

Through the sobbing and the tears and snot rolling down my face, something clicked. I *heard* that voice. I heard the voice producing all these what-ifs as if it were my voice but not really mine.

Now I'm competitive and had not really learned the grace of losing very well. The thought of this other voice beating me, that I was not in control, turned anguish into anger. *How dare these thoughts win! I am the master, not you, Mean Little Voice.*

I slowly uncurled from the fetal position, sat up, and started to dissect all the what-ifs. I really had been making up all these thoughts. The sobbing stopped. Well, it reduced to more of a whimper. I just stared at her. She was right. I had let the Mean Little Voice completely take over, rendering me useless. It was then that I vowed not to let the Mean Little Voice win anymore. And this vow has served me well throughout most of my life. Except when it didn't.

INSTINCT, INTUITION, AND THE COUSINS

We all have inner monologues. We tell ourselves that we are hungry, need to go to the bathroom, or are tired. From an early age, these basic instincts have ensured that our bodies continue to function. Instincts are also tied to our fight, flight, or freeze responses. These physiological reactions occur to counter a perceived harmful event, attack, or threat to survival. Our instincts form the foundation that keeps us alive and safe.

As we grew older, matured, and experienced more of the world, we developed intuition. Instincts are basic to survival. Intuition gathers information through our senses (sight, sound, and so on), synthesizes them, and makes decisions based on those experiences to keep us safe. "That stove looks hot; I shouldn't touch it." Or have you ever been walking along and saw a dark alley, and something inside you said, "Don't go down there"? That's our intuition speaking up, and like instinct, we listen to it to keep ourselves safe. It's the reason we don't run out into a busy street; our intuition tells us that it's dangerous, and we might end up dead.

From instincts and intuition have grown other "voices." Two of them are nefarious: the Mean Little Voice and the Sneaky Little Bastard. I will refer to them as the Cousins (like my cousins, they have the same middle name).

The Mean Little Voice is just that—mean. After my catastrophic breakup with Russell, that Mean Little Voice spewed all types of lies.

- *I'm not good enough.*
- *Russell never loved me because I'm unlovable.*
- *I'm undatable.*
- *I'm worthless.*

What I call the Mean Little Voice goes by many names. Some

people call it the inner critic, the troll, the impostor, or the saboteur. In the end, they're all the same.

Its cousin, the Sneaky Little Bastard, is a little harder to perceive, which is what makes it so sneaky. Have you ever had a task that you know is going to be hard to do and think, *I'll just do it tomorrow,* or *I should go clean out the dishwasher now*? That is the Sneaky Little Bastard. You may say, "That's just procrastinating." But in this scenario, it is more than that.

The Cousins were conceived out of our instincts and intuition to protect and keep us safe. But safe from what?

The Cousins were conceived out of our instincts and intuition to protect and keep us safe. But safe from what?

After my breakup with Russell, the Mean Little Voice was trying to keep me safe from having my heart broken again. If I believed I was unlovable and worthless, I would never have to venture out again, never put myself out into the world, never have to make myself vulnerable, only to have my heart broken and go through those awful feelings again.

Our brains have devised these voices to protect our fragile little egos. Though they want you to think that they are trying to be helpful, they aren't. They are stopping you from trying new things and moving on.

Let's take impostor syndrome,* for example. Impostor syndrome is the feeling that you are not worthy, you aren't good

---

* Interesting fact: you may have also seen this spelled as *imposter* syndrome. Both imposter and impostor are correct, but the more technically and clinically correct term is impostor, which you will see throughout the book.

enough, or you are a fraud. The Cousins will stop you from trying new things or going for a raise or promotion because of these self-doubts. For those who fear failure, the Cousins protect you from starting something so there is no way to experience future failure. And the converse is true. If you fear success, they stop you from trying, and you never have a chance to succeed.

Because the Mean Little Voice and the Sneaky Little Bastard have also grown out of our instincts and intuition and have the same fundamental goal of keeping you safe, figuring out which voice is speaking might be difficult. But once you recognize the Cousins, it's easier to shut them down.

WHAT DO YOU MEAN, THE COUSINS SPEAK TO YOU?

Look, maybe I'm not completely normal. And maybe I've spent my whole life taking for granted that I could recognize the voices for what they are. I was fortunate to have a mom who enabled me to recognize the differences at an early age. You might not have had a mom like mine or a comparable situation. So if it is difficult to tell the difference between instinct, intuition, and the malevolent voices, that's probably normal. You're normal.

Until this point, you may have never thought about these two characters living in your mind. The Mean Little Voice and the Sneaky Little Bastard will sound different to different people. As such, you might experience them differently than I do. I recently held a workshop and asked people what their Mean Little Voice sounded like. I had a range of answers, like it was a *Sleepy Hollow* type of whisper or a mean girl. And one person said it sounded like a nagging mother. My Mean Little Voice is a lot easier to detect. Getting dumped before the CATOICO dance served me well because it helped me identify it and recognize it my whole life. Its words are edgy and sound a bit oily.

On the other hand, my Sneaky Little Bastard sounds ordinary. It's like I am having a normal conversation with myself. *Should I eat now or after I finish my next conference call? Should I finally approach that new client, or is now a good time to clean my office?* In my head, that voice sounds the same. In the first example, that was instinct telling me I'm hungry and should really think about eating. In the second example, while cleaning my office would be a good thing, that Sneaky Little Bastard steered me away from doing something that was outside my comfort zone. At first that sounds like procrastination. But the voice's motive makes the difference. Deciding to eat later is procrastination. Deciding to put off a task because deep down you are afraid that you are stretching yourself by trying something new, that there is a possibility it might go wrong, or that you will be rejected are all signs of the Sneaky Little Bastard. Instead of sitting down and doing the challenging work, it is sometimes easier to just clean the house.

The Sneaky Little Bastard also preys on those of us who are perfectionists or obsessive-compulsive about our work. We hold onto it, hoping to get it to that 100 percent perfect mark, never realizing that the mark will always be out of our reach. Even if we think we are close, we find some new way to start over, rehash, or change our work. The Sneaky Little Bastard has a heyday with this type of behavior. It's the one whispering in your ear, *That's pretty good, but it's not ready yet. Let's keep going.*

LET ME SAVE YOU THE TIME: WHAT HASN'T WORKED

There is something to be said about the power of positive thinking. According to research performed by Dr. Claire Eagleson and her team, replacing negative thoughts with positive imagery had minor effects, suggesting that any form of positive ideas can be used to effectively counter worry. But it can only get you so far.

I was in a craft store the other day picking up some holiday decorations. I wandered down a few aisles and found all these wooden signs: "You got this." "Go get 'em today." "Believe." I remember when I was going through some of my internal battles, I would say to myself, "I can do it; I can do it." I thought that by saying this over and over, it would make it true.

I hoped the Mean Little Voice would listen to the mantras and just say *OK, she wins*, roll over, and die. That didn't happen. No matter how many times I said to myself "I can do it," I wondered if it was true because I wasn't sure if I genuinely believed it.

I call these wooden signs and surficial mantras bland affirmations. They are the icing on a moldy cake. If sweet and sugary, they might initially make us feel good. But the actual cake is rotten. No matter how much icing you put on that cake, it will not make the cake better. I'm a hobbyist baker; it's pretty obvious that you always start with the cake and then put on the icing.

> **The worst means of coping with the voices is to shove them down deep and overcompensate.**

Some people acknowledge their voices and just move on. For many, this works well because the volume of the voices is not that great, and it's easy to assess whether they are rational and to shut them down and keep moving forward. However, when the stakes get higher, the voices can grow louder, and it's more difficult to assess their validity and ultimately, reject them. Those who are in this camp never truly deal with why the voices are coming up in the first place. The voices will continue to recur and, over time, gain a little more footing with each pass.

The worst means of coping with the voices is to shove them down deep and overcompensate.

I have a few friends who have taken this track. Believing the voices, they tell themselves, "I'm not good enough, so I'm going to do more to prove that I am." They are always overly busy trying to prove to the world—but more importantly, to themselves—that they are worthy. By shoving these feelings down and not dealing with them, they begin to fester. Over time, these friends begin to experience anxiety, burnout, uncertainty, and sometimes depression. They are disappointed, dissatisfied, or even angry with themselves. Moreover, they are always looking for validation for their lives.

The good news is that there is a way out of these situations. But it takes a willingness to want to turn things around, quiet the voices, and find a better version of who you are.

THE COMFORTABLE LIFE, OR STRETCHING FOR SOMETHING MORE

At Texas A&M University, I fell in love with ocean engineering (basically civil engineering but add water). When it came time to graduate, I looked at all my classmates who were excited to head to Houston and start the next chapter of their lives working for some big company. I couldn't do it. I was too rambunctious and had a zeal to see the world. So what did I do? I joined the

US Navy. The navy served me well, crisscrossing me across the globe from Guam to Puerto Rico, to Okinawa and Alaska, gaining experience in engineering, meeting new people, and immersing myself in different cultures. Through all this, there was a tickle in the back of my brain that at some point in my life, I wanted to be an entrepreneur.

After six years of active duty, I joined the naval reserves. But this wasn't the right time to become an entrepreneur because, quite frankly, I had no idea what I wanted to do or how the civilian business world worked. I needed experience. Taking my love of engineering and building to the construction industry, I absorbed every piece of information possible. Knowing there was more to learn, I went back to school, and during my master's and PhD programs, I took an elective class in entrepreneurship. I even went so far as to create my corporation in 2006, JL Donahue Engineering, Inc. I know, super-original name, but I was proud of my little business.

After graduate school, I was recalled to active duty for fourteen months, which included a tour in Iraq. Then, on returning to civilian life, I debated whether to strike out as an entrepreneur or go to work for an established engineering firm. I took the safer route and decided to work at a highly regarded company. I just didn't feel ready or that it was the right time for me to go out on my own.

The lifestyle I enjoyed while working at this medium-sized company for several years was nice. I had an office in San Francisco, on Market Street, and could look out my window and see Alcatraz on days that weren't fogged in. The people I worked with were wonderful. I had a nice, consistent paycheck. I also had a sizable mortgage. But after a few years, colleagues were owning businesses, and I started to grow a bit jealous. If they could do it, so could I.

Going out on my own as an entrepreneur, being my own boss, was something that I knew I could do. The Mean Little Voice had been lying dormant for years but started to awaken. The what-ifs started again.

What if I can't make it work?
What if I can't provide for my family?
What if we lose the mortgage? Where would we live?
What if I need to go groveling back for my job?
What if . . .
What if . . .
What if . . .

Then, my Mean Little Voice tag-teamed with my Sneaky Little Bastard. I started to rationalize just staying put.

Why can't I just be happy where I am?
It's not so bad.
Look at the view from my office!

The voices home in on our perceived vulnerabilities, weaknesses, and doubts. Because they are a part of us, they know our flaws, even the ones we don't want to acknowledge.

> **The voices home in on our perceived vulnerabilities, weaknesses, and doubts. Because they are a part of us, they know our flaws, even the ones we don't want to acknowledge.**

They zero in and exploit those weaknesses. The voices had a field day with my perceived weaknesses: selling myself, performing accounting or tricky IT work, feeling smart enough, and being bold and courageous enough.

Luckily, I started to recall my mother's words: "Are you going to let them win?" *Dang it. She's right. I'm an engineer and pretty darn organized. I can figure this out.*

The wise words of my mother rang true for me from the last of my high school years through my twenties and thirties and into my forties. That simple phrase "Are you going to let them win?" would shine like a beacon in my head when it was clouded with doubts, procrastination, and the unending what-ifs. It would ground me every single time. Sometimes it would take a while for that beacon to light up, but once it did, problems began to resolve themselves. The more it happened, the quicker my response would be. Actively recognizing the voices, I would shut them down.

That was, until Afghanistan.

UNTIL A SIMPLE MANTRA ISN'T ENOUGH

There may be points in your life when it is impossible to discern the voices of instinct and intuition from those of the Mean Little Voice and the Sneaky Little Bastard. This often happens when your life is careening out of control. Too much trauma, stress, chaos, busyness, and pressure cloud your mind, and the beacon can't shine through. Those words of wisdom become too faint, and you can't hear them through all the noise. For me, the noise was war.

During my tour in Afghanistan as the commanding officer (CO) of the battalion, I faced the highest stakes of my life. Back on active duty, I was the CO of a battalion of over six hundred US Navy Seabees. The Seabees are land-based units that provide horizontal and vertical construction, such as building bases, reconstructing roads, drilling water wells, and repairing bridges. The stress and hazards were so high that my mom's words of wisdom were not enough. I couldn't shut down my Mean Little Voice and Sneaky Little Bastard, and too often, I was swayed by their constant commentary.

In Afghanistan, our traditional tasking included maintaining and building bases for the United States and other NATO countries. We also had the task of training the newly formed Afghan engineer unit because to be sustainable, every military unit needs engineers to build roads, maintain bases, drill water wells, and operate heavy construction machinery.

If you try to understand the command structure of the military, it's confusing. As a US Navy battalion, half of my personnel were with me in Kabul but reported to a US Army brigade; the other half was under the Special Forces umbrella down in Bagram. So it starts weird because the battalion is split in two, but I maintain the responsibility for all members.

My boss was an army colonel (an O6), one rank above me; I was a navy commander (an O5). Now there are bad bosses, and then there was the colonel. He was about six feet, seven inches tall and probably weighed about 280 pounds. He was enormous; I only came up to his shoulder. He was hotheaded and vicious. He yelled and belittled anyone and everything in meetings. Luckily, I was in Kabul, and he was about an hour's helicopter ride south in Bagram. It was so common for him to rip people to shreds in the biweekly update meetings that I started to make tick marks on my dry-erase board every time it happened. No one wanted to speak. No one wanted to make even the tiniest mistake. The toxic environment permeated his staff and the units that served under him. Officers were soon turning on other officers, pointing fingers, and backstabbing each other to avoid his wrath in meetings. He threatened to fire me three or four times because I messed up somehow or he didn't agree with my decisions. Even his staff decided to defect and created excuses to perform "inspections" on our battalion, so they could come hang out in Kabul for a couple of weeks.

I endured a lot on that deployment. Every time I got on a helicopter to check on my Seabees at other bases, we were shot at. You see, we flew at night, and if you looked out the back of the helicopter, you could see the tracer rounds of the enemy gunfire behind you. Suicide bombers attempted to blow up our base. Colleagues were killed in ambushes while on convoys in Kabul. I even had an assassination attempt on my life. Here's the wild part. Through all that, the colonel was the enemy! The continuous daily bombardment, the threat of being fired at the slightest trivial misstep, and the mental abuse began to wear at me. I kept thinking, *Do not let him beat you.*

Nearing the end of the deployment, he asked if I was going for another job in command, and I said no. I was mentally and physically tired. I had been a CO for three years and needed a chance to recharge. His reply was laced with venom: "Good. You aren't ready at all." It stung. Then he laid bare what he really thought of me.

In addition to the colonel, I had five bosses in Bahrain and the United States. Five! Each had their own style and agenda. I know many of you can commiserate with this situation.

Two weeks before redeploying home, the inspector general informed me that I had racked up fifty-four grievances. In the military, you can send in an anonymous complaint called a grievance. Most battalions receive five to ten, but not a staggering fifty-four. My administrative affairs boss immediately labeled me a "shit-bird." What kind of battalion was I running that would have so many complaints? What had I done to run the morale of the battalion into the ground? I wondered as well.

Turns out, two people sent in all those complaints, not fifty-four people making just one. Almost all of them were petty and against their immediate supervisor, who was three tiers below me. Grievances count against the battalion, not the individual, and as the CO, I represent the battalion. Ergo, they counted against me.

Then a week before leaving Afghanistan, one of my Seabees needed to return to the United States earlier than everyone else. He flew out of Afghanistan to the way station in Sembach, Germany. Technically, he was still assigned to the battalion but now attached to another unit until he had a scheduled flight to Norfolk, Virginia. While in Germany, he took his life. I was gutted. He was a well-known and well-liked individual, as well as one of our go-to guys in the Operations Department.

The military takes suicide very seriously. The investigation and reports went to the highest levels of the navy. Because he was still assigned to my battalion, it was now my fault. My administrative boss was furious. First there were the grievances, and now a suicide in less than two weeks. I later found out that he called one of the other bosses and threatened to relieve me of duty immediately. In other words, fire me.

When we arrived in the United States, all my bosses and bosses' bosses knew about the suicide and apparent problems with morale in the battalion due to the number of grievances. My administrative boss went as far as to tell me I had killed that Seabee. "His blood is on your hands." Those words still haunt me. I know it's not true, but there remains a scar that someone would think so little of me to tell me that I am basically a murderer.

They allowed me to have my change of command and not be fired. But just because I gave the reins to someone else didn't mean it was over. I was repeatedly questioned as the investigations into the grievances and the suicide went on for months.

After four long, anguish-filled months, I was cleared of all wrongdoing. All the grievances were found to be unwarranted. The suicide occurred while the Seabee was attached to a different unit, one over which I had no oversight.

I was cleared and nothing would go on my record. As is typical, after everything I had gone through, I was told, "Continue as normal." But at that point, I would never be able to go back to normal. I remember sitting with my husband for his birthday dinner. I tried to be cheerful, but it wasn't genuine. I didn't deserve this wonderful, giving, supportive, lively person in my life.

Where once I had that shining beacon of my mom's words illuminating the darkness in my head, it failed. I couldn't even say the words anymore. They were useless, just like I felt. I had put every piece of my soul into the job and done my best to hold it all together. But the circumstances kept piling on and piling on until they had beaten me. The Mean Little Voice set up permanent residence in my head. It even picked out potted plants and ordered cable TV. That tour shattered all sense of self that I had once been. The upbeat, positive, caring person I had been was gone, leaving a bitter, angry, and empty person behind.

In your life, there will be times when life piles it on. You receive a poor performance review, there is great disruption in your home life, or things don't go as planned at work. You keep disappointing people, even if it isn't your fault. You struggle to keep your head above water. One thing after another. We've all been there.

I didn't want to hurt anymore. I didn't want to be plagued with constant feelings of inadequacy. I just wanted to be myself again, that slightly brash, confident officer. But most importantly, I wanted to be the happy person I once was.

To piece myself back together, I pulled examples from what the military taught us about physical enemies and applied that knowledge to the ones lounging around and taking up too much space in my head.

THE WARRIOR FRAMEWORK

The Warrior Framework is deceptively simple, yet powerful. Adopting the Warrior Mindset is about wanting something so badly that you are ready to earn it. In the case of my Afghanistan tour, I no longer wanted to be languishing. It was draining my mental health and starting to take a toll on my physical health. I decided I no longer wanted to sit on the sidelines and let the Cousins rule my well-being.

I needed a way out of this, so I fell back on my knowledge and military training. Although I am an engineer, and the navy trained me to build in all types of environments, I was also taught how to defend myself. The Seabee motto is “We Build, We Fight.” When in a hostile environment, we have a very rigid process, the rules of cngagement, when dealing with an enemy. The rules of engagement outline the circumstances and limitations to initiate or continue combat. The sequence starts with vigilance and observing the world around you, gaining something often called situational awareness. Next, if a person or car is coming toward you, we assess whether they are friends or foes. If friend, cool. Carry on with what you were doing. If foe, ready yourself. If the enemy keeps coming, use the appropriate amount of force to repel them.

The Warrior Framework is deceptively simple, yet powerful.

This sequence is ingrained into every troop over and over: Perceive, Assess, Ready, Act. We train this sequence in simulations and field exercises. It must become second nature because in an actual situation, it should only take two to five seconds. If you must think about what's next, it's too late.

I had found that just recognizing the Mean Little Voice was no longer enough to make it go away and leave me alone. I began to wonder, since this sequence could work against physical enemies, could it work against my mental enemies as well? In my mind, I had only been doing the first two steps of the sequence, Perceive and Assess. That's all that was needed earlier in life. But what would the third and fourth steps, Ready and Act, look like?

In the real world, the Ready step entails telling the enemy to back off. Methods for this might include flashing lights, using hand signals, or shooting flares at an oncoming vehicle or person to tell them to stay away. If they keep coming, you prepare yourself and your weapon for conflict. But how could I tell my thoughts to go away? Shooting myself with a flare obviously wasn't practical. I needed a counterpoint to yell at my Mean Little Voice to "halt!" I knew such a counterpoint dwelled somewhere inside me, but it wasn't saying much these days. The counterpoint needed to be stronger. It needed to have a bigger voice and to become a warrior to defeat the voices seeking to ruin all that I had left.

I knew I had to act. I was so tired of what I had become. I needed to find a new way over, through, or around the obstacles that I was creating in my mind. I wanted to be happy and regain some of my confidence, so I needed to figure out how to get there.

Over the next several months, I thought about, hashed, rehashed, scrapped, and finally developed the Warrior Framework I present to you in Figure 1.1. It turns out that applying a century or more of military tactics to a mental enemy is possible. The four steps used in the physical world can be used in the metaphysical one as well. The four steps remain straightforward, though implementation takes practice and a will to want more from yourself.

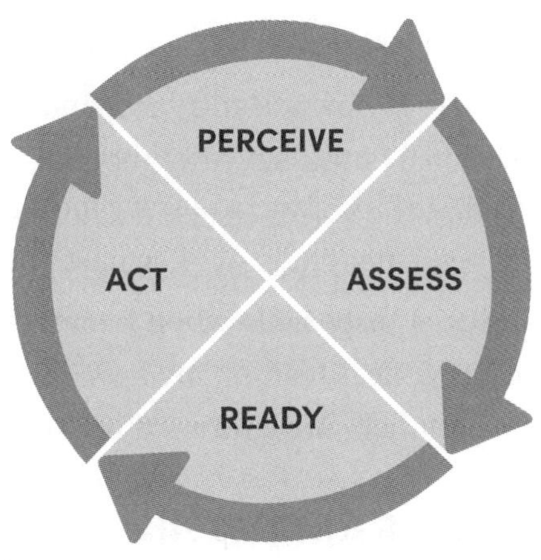

FIGURE 1.1. THE WARRIOR FRAMEWORK

1. Perceive: Recognize your thoughts.
2. Assess: Distinguish between instinct, intuition, and your inner critic.
3. Ready: Engage your counterpoint, the warrior.
4. Act: Take that first step.

Since 2016, I have been using this framework whenever I hear the little voices.

Are you sure you can do this?
No one will listen.
Who do you think you are?
Who cares what you have to say?
We don't have to do this now.

At first, it was difficult. I'd get through steps 1 and 2 but struggle with step 3. But just as we're relentlessly trained in the military, I decided to train my brain to engage the counterpoint and then act. Each time I used the framework, it got a little easier and faster.

The voices soon died down from a cacophony to mere shouts and then the occasional outbursts. After months, my head finally began to clear. Today, the voices speak in a normal tone; there's no yelling. Notice that I did not say that I got rid of the voices. I still hear them speak, especially when I am trying something outside my comfort zone. I lean on my training, counter them, shut them down, and then move forward with certainty.

VALUE IN THE FRAMEWORK

As I mentioned earlier, besides the obviousness of quieting the voices, the framework was beneficial for both my mental and physical well-being. Unchecked, the voices would creep in and start causing self-doubt, stress, and anxiety. I started to withdraw from society, not taking my friends' calls, staying in bed in the dark, and becoming a shell of a human being to my spouse.

Mental stress can manifest itself in physical effects over time, such as increased heart rate, higher blood pressure, shortness of breath, muscle aches, and insomnia. How do I know this? Besides doing a lot of clinical research on the subject, this was me for about six months. Then the Warrior Framework helped me to find myself again.

Imagine being able to master the voices in your head. When they pop up, you recognize them, assess if they are friend or foe, knock them down, and move forward. Heck, by the end of this book, you may even embrace them. But let's not get ahead of ourselves.

Imagine being in a place in your life where you don't feel like you need to become a different version of yourself just to be accepted because you know you are enough.

Imagine being able to reach your goals and objectives faster. With each cycle through the framework, you get quicker and more confident. Smaller tasks are easily completed, and you are ready to take that first step with confidence along a well-defined path forward. Larger, more daunting goals are broken into manageable tasks, and you feel in the flow as you start to check off your list one by one.

I want you to ask yourself these four questions. And if the answer to any of these is yes, this is the book for you:

1. Am I unhappy with where I am today?
2. Do I feel like I am capable of more?
3. Do I know deep down that I can do great things?
4. Am I ready to try new tactics and do the work to reach my goal?

By the end of this book, you will have the tools to move past whatever is holding you back and progress into your potential.

I want you to do something for me. It's easy. All it takes is a pen and a sticky note. If you don't have a sticky note, that's OK. Just grab a piece of paper.

WARRIOR EXERCISE

Write down one goal that you would like to conquer or at least start by the end of this book.

____

____

____

It can be big, like making a huge life decision. Or it can be small, like taking up a new hobby. What is your goal? Write it on the sticky note and put it on your desk. That's it.

THE SCIENCE OF STICKIES

You may be thinking, *Well, I know what it is, so I don't actually have to write it down.* I am asking for a small amount of faith. Writing your goal down has more to do with science and the way your brain works. Researchers have found that the unique, complex, spatial, and tactile information associated with writing by hand on physical paper is what leads to improved memory. Writing things down improves what the brain calls coding. No, not Java, Python, or C++. This type of coding occurs in the hippocampus, the section of the brain that deals with memory retention. The act of writing things down starts to rewire our brain. According to a study by Dr. Gail Matthews of the Dominican University of California, people who wrote down their goals were 42 percent more likely to achieve them than those who simply thought about them.

You may also say, "I'll just write it on my phone." OK, while this is better than nothing, Professor Kuniyoshi Sakai, a neuroscientist from the University of Tokyo, found that writing things down on paper can lead to stronger brain activity and better memory recall than using a digital device. Let's give ourselves the best fighting chance possible. Find a sticky note or a plain old piece of paper.

> **People who wrote down their goals were 42 percent more likely to achieve them than those who simply thought about them.**

I realize that some of you

may be reading this on a tablet or other electronic device. In this case, if possible, still find a sticky. If not, I recommend opening a notes app and writing it there.

Throughout the book, I refer to that little sticky on your desk. The effects of visualization have been studied by numerous prominent scientists. That little sticky has already helped you to solidify the goal in your mind and has given you a clear target to work toward. Visualizing your written goals can significantly boost motivation, engagement, and accountability. When you see your goals written down, it creates a sense of commitment. So give it a try.

In the next chapter, we look at some reasons we aren't moving forward. We'll uncover some of the uncomfortable truths we don't want to admit. You might see yourselves in the examples: "Yep, that's me." But don't worry. You've got this, and I am right there with you at every step. You've already completed your first task and this first chapter. Your little sticky will become your lifeline as we start to wade into the murky realm of the what-ifs.

WARRIOR DEBRIEF

1. The voice of your inner critic may sound the same as the voices of the basic instincts and intuition that are designed to keep you safe, which is why we trust it without question.
2. The Mean Little Voice and the Sneaky Little Bastard have grown out of instinct and intuition, but they are typically negative, irrational, and stop you from moving forward.
3. The Warrior Framework (Perceive, Assess, Ready, Act) is designed to help you recognize, assess, and counter negative inner voices, enabling you to take positive action and achieve your goals.
4. Writing down your goals improves memory retention and increases the likelihood of achieving them, as supported by scientific research.

2

THE WHAT-IFS—PERCEIVE

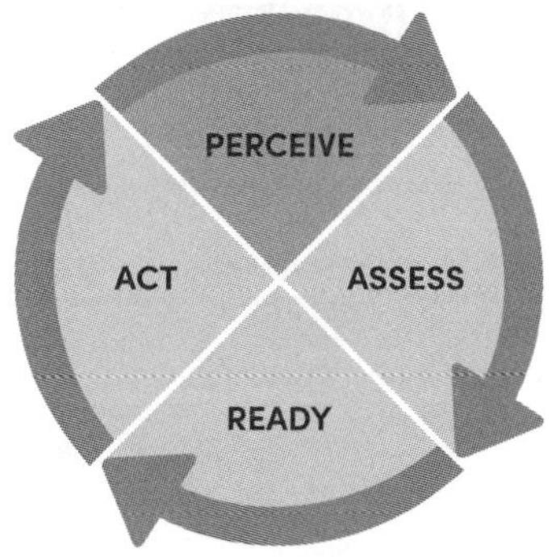

The first step in creating a Warrior Framework is Perceive. We need to learn how to pay attention to the comments and the questions of our inner monologues. As you work through the chapter, you'll discover that you're not alone. So many others struggle with how they see themselves or perceptions of their future selves.

How many times have you asked yourself, "What if I'm a fraud?" "What if I fail?" "What if I succeed?" As you might guess, these three what-ifs are the calling cards for impostor syndrome, the fear of failure, and the fear of success, respectively.

While there may be other pertinent what-ifs out there, these three constitute the reasons we hold ourselves back from going after a goal, a dream, or an objective. They are the repeatable opening monologues of the Mean Little Voice and Sneaky Little Bastard. I have found that the best way to determine if the voices are instinct, intuition, or the Cousins is to pay attention to the questions I ask myself.

You may not relate to all three, but there are common traits between them, as seen in Figure 2.1. The what-ifs often have deeper, nastier meanings that originate from our innate insecurities and disbelief in ourselves.

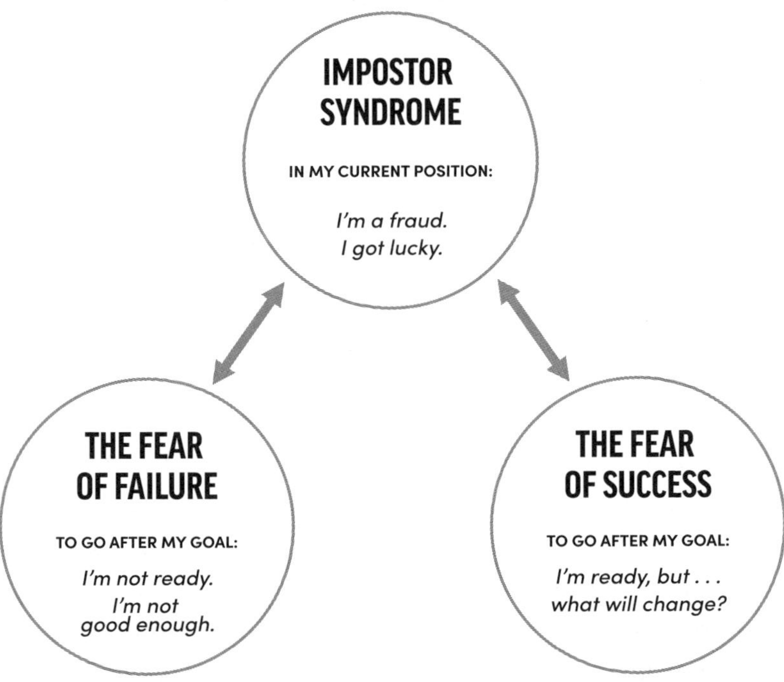

FIGURE 2.1. THE INTERPLAY BETWEEN IMPOSTOR SYNDROME, THE FEAR OF FAILURE, AND THE FEAR OF SUCCESS

"WHAT IF I'M A FRAUD?": IMPOSTOR SYNDROME

Over the course of my life, I've had the opportunity to meet and befriend several extraordinary people. One of them is Michelle, a fellow keynote speaker, author, and veteran. I recently asked her about her experiences with impostor syndrome, and she relayed the story of her first duty station with the US Air Force.

Michelle sat in the cockpit of the F-16 reviewing the instrument panel. For her, they all had meaning, but to the rest of the world, it looked like an alphabet soup of dials, levers, and knobs. Being selected to fly jets for the US Air Force had always been her dream, and here she was, making her last-minute checks.

The fighter squadron she belonged to was tough. Sure, she made it through the initial training, but here in Japan, flying at Mach 1 was taking it up a notch. There was no room for error. The slightest miscalculation could mean death—of yourself, of your teammates, or of those on the ground. As a new F-16 pilot, Michelle was trying to find her footing in a new and difficult career field where reputation was everything.

Either you cut it, or you're out.

The stress was relentless. "I had a false narrative when I became an F-16 pilot," Michelle told me. "In my early training, I was consumed by chasing down that goal, working insane hours. Every ounce of my energy was going into learning to become a pilot, competing to get that fighter jet." And she had beaten the odds and made it happen. But when she reached her goal, it was harder than she thought. "I used to tell myself, 'I've made it. I should know what I'm doing.'" In truth, it was very much the opposite.

She felt like such an impostor in that squadron. Always trying to fit in with the guys and trying to be the best. And Michelle had the same thoughts that most people with impostor syndrome experience:

I'm still not good enough.
I'm a fake.
I've only gotten lucky so far.
I must train harder.

She put additional stress on herself when she realized the inherent pressure of being one of the few female pilots. Other pilots would do a double take when a woman walked into the room because there were only two of them in the whole squadron. "There's this feeling that any failure highlights women negatively, and you're setting the reputation for all female fighter pilots." She felt as though she had to be supertough and prove that she deserved to be there more than anyone else because command was already watching her. She wanted to do the best she could, but she also wanted to fit in and show no signs of weakness.

For months that little voice in the back of her head would sneak in. *What are you doing here? Do you really think you're as good as these guys?*

Maybe being more like them, laughing at their jokes, talking about football—which she had zero interest in—would help her blend in.

Reflecting, Michelle said she wished she had gone into the situation realizing that she was a beginner, and this would be hard. And that it was OK to be willing to ask questions and ask for help. She wished she had a healthier mindset of curiosity so she could be a sponge for knowledge.

Instead, the voices got stronger.

Oh crap. I don't think I'm cut out to be here.
I don't think I have the aptitude to do this.
I'm not the type of person that is going to do well in this career.

Her descent on the spiral of impostor syndrome began. When challenged, she took what should have been a normal level of doubt to questioning her self-worth and identity.

What she hadn't yet realized is that everyone in the squadron had gone through the same thing: "I lost my perspective that what I was going through was normal for a fighter pilot."

Michelle struggled during those first two years at the combat squadron. But approaching the end of that first assignment, she began to question her life choices. She realized she could not live like that for her ten-year commitment to the US Air Force. She wouldn't be able to operate under that level of stress and pressure while needing to perform perfectly.

Michelle got to a point of such despair that she knew she needed a change, any change. When the time came to switch squadrons and move to Texas, she knew this was a chance to start over, maybe even start from scratch.

She decided to be herself around her fellow pilots. No more talk about football. An enthusiastic fan of nonconventional sports like mountaineering and rock climbing, she found three or four other pilots, all guys, in her squadron who liked those things too. She had found her people and created a new supportive network.

More importantly, Michelle took a few steps back to gain perspective on how naive she believed she had been at her first squadron. This moment to reset allowed her to see how in the weeds she had been. She took on that curiosity mindset she so wished she had adopted early on and started asking questions and for help when needed. Her flying improved dramatically. Michelle Curran was later selected as the second woman to fly in the coveted Lead Solo position for the US Air Force Thunderbirds!

A vicious Mean Little Voice continually questioned Michelle's worthiness of being a fighter pilot. The stress and self-doubt brought her to a point of such despair that she almost quit and robbed the world of a great pilot.

The Core of Impostor Syndrome

The acknowledgment and acceptance of impostor syndrome have recently become more mainstream. Once only talked about in hushed tones with a therapist, this is a topic more and more people publicly acknowledge they have struggled with.

People who experience impostor syndrome feel they will never be good enough, that they don't belong, or that they are fakes, and it's only a matter of time before everyone sees right through them.

I've also noticed that once people hear about and understand what impostor syndrome is, there is a realization and an aha moment. An acknowledgment of "Yes, that's what I have been feeling, but I ever knew there was a name for it." As you see the light of realization in their eyes, you also see their shoulders relax.

> People who experience impostor syndrome feel they will never be good enough, that they don't belong, or that they are fakes, and it's only a matter of time before everyone sees right through them. If this is what you're experiencing, you have convinced yourself that you are an impostor.

"You mean there are others out there like me? I'm not alone?"

Impostor syndrome was first studied by Dr. Pauline Clance and Dr. Suzanne Imes in 1978. Their test group included over 150 women and was composed of students recognized for their academic excellence and extraordinarily successful and respected women from various fields. Through their research, they postulated that "women who experience the impostor phenomenon maintain a strong belief that they are not intelligent: in fact, they are convinced that they have fooled anyone who thinks otherwise."

As someone who has impostor syndrome from time to time, it's tough for me to read the women's comments:

"I'm not good enough to be on the faculty here. Some mistake was made in the selection process."

"Obviously I'm in this position because my abilities have been overestimated."

"I was convinced that I would be discovered as a phony when I took my comprehensive doctoral examination. In one way, I was somewhat relieved at this prospect because the pretense would finally be over."

Who wants to show up to work like this every day?

Impostor syndrome can rob you of the joy of what you've achieved. Many of the test subjects reported anxiety, a lack of self-confidence, and depression. Almost all the test subjects were frustrated by the inability to meet their self-imposed standards of achievement. Let me repeat that: *self-imposed*. The participants had met the standards of the university or professional field and were admired by others, but their self-doubts led to feelings of incompetence. They believed they had gotten to their positions by pretending to be smart and getting lucky.

Clance and Imes performed only preliminary research on men, which proved inconclusive. For quite some time, it was thought in the psychology community that impostor syndrome was something only women dealt with. Over the years, as research continued, the subject of who is affected by impostor syndrome shifted from just women to any high-performing individuals. Today, we realize impostor syndrome is experienced in people in all walks of life. It doesn't discriminate; old people, young people, men, women, rich, or poor, the common traits remain. You don't feel like you have lived up to your self-imposed standards, and you are in your position by accident.

I've had my bouts of impostor syndrome even as I'm authoring this book. The Mean Little Voice keeps whispering, *What do you know about writing books? You're an engineer and hate writing. Nobody is going to read it.*

Even the Sneaky Little Bastard came to the party. *You don't really have to hit your word count goals today. Let's create some spreadsheets. That's much more fun.*

I've had colleagues in the navy not go for their dream jobs, which they were qualified for because, until that point, they felt they were just lucky and would have to try even harder to keep up with appearances if they got the job.

Those who have expressed impostor syndrome worry that their colleagues will see them for what and who *they believe* they are rather than what the truth is. They may also believe that others think more highly of them than they think of themselves.

But what about situations like that of Michelle, the trailblazer, where you feel like you might need to work harder, better, or longer hours just to prove to yourself that you are worthy? Like Michelle, in my career, and as typically the only woman in the room, I was never told that I needed to do so, yet there was always that voice in my head telling me it needed to be done. Is there an unwritten rule that those in similar positions need to work harder to gain respect, or did we make it all up in our heads? I believe that it can be a bit of both, depending on the situation. Look, there will always be those people who demand more of you because you might be different in some way. But dealing with them is the subject of a different book. Let's deal with ourselves first.

Many of us consciously or unconsciously put the mantle of working harder to be respected on ourselves. That's when we start to compare ourselves to others and set the *self-imposed* bar of worthiness so high that if we could reach it, we would prove that we were beyond question by the naysayers. We will have earned the ability to not be labeled as a fluke or lucky. Anything less is a failure. What we fail to realize is that other influences affect our sense of self. TV, social media, magazines, and even our mentors and idols contribute to how we see our current self and where we want to be.

I've also had readers and clients ask, "What about just faking it till you make it?" For many with impostor syndrome, this is like hitting the big red "Easy" button. You may feel in over your head or clueless about how you are supposed to function in your position. "I'll just pretend I know what I'm doing until I convince everyone around me that I do."

I do not espouse this philosophy. Read these next few words and take them to heart. You have been put in the new position because someone believes in you—believes in you so much that he or she promoted you. You earned the right to be there. Corporations and associations do not like risk. They would not have put you there unless you deserved it. Realize that you are *not* faking it for the benefit of those around you. Rather, you are faking it until you believe it yourself. So let's start with belief in ourselves. Keep reading. I've got some helpful tips for this.

Thomas is a programmer at a start-up human capital management firm. Although he has worked in industry for twelve years, he does not have a degree in computer science and is not a natural-born coder, so he feels less competent than the newer, younger programmers recently brought into the company. Last year, at the annual retreat, he was nominated for an MVP award. His initial reaction was shock. The person who nominated him came by and proudly said, "I nominated you. I appreciate what you did on this project and your effort and everything. You deserve that recognition."

Thomas's first thought was, *Oh no. I'm just here. I'm just doing my job*. Usually, his first instinct is to automatically say, "Thank you," but he always seems to shy away from recognition. Even the CEO of the company came up to him and told him what an impressive job he had done that year. Thomas responded that the nomination meant a lot, especially to hear it from him. But he still has that ache in his chest and the nagging question in his mind: *Is this for real?*

Impostor Syndrome Is Not About Being Humble

There is a difference between being humble and having impostor syndrome. Being humble is owning your achievements but not being braggadocious about them. Sure, I have a PhD, but I don't go around introducing myself as Dr. Donahue. No, it's simply Jenn.

In comparison, impostor syndrome does not recognize your achievements.

In comparison, impostor syndrome does not recognize your achievements. You could have a slew of acronyms after your name and still feel like you will never be enough for yourself or for the world.

Being humble is also about dutifully saying "Thank you" when someone compliments you and recognizing the sincerity in those two words. For those with impostor syndrome, a compliment often makes them cringe. Or they downplay their actions. Imagine someone telling you how great you did on a project, and your response is something like, "Oh, anyone could do it." Though it is an attempt to downplay your actions and take the spotlight off you, the response insults the person who gave you the compliment. That person went out of his or her way to recognize the magnificent work you had done. Yet your response made the effort and sincerity seem trivial and worthless.

Impostor Syndrome and Social Media: It's Not Just the Young Kids

Impostor syndrome often rears its ugly head when we compare ourselves to others. We have all heard the news and seen reports about the impact of social media and the increase in impostor syndrome, especially on teens and twenty-year-olds. Their influencer idols post filtered yet glamorous photos and videos of their lives—what to wear this season, the latest trends in fitness, and exotic vacation locales. Life looks perfect. As they scroll through images of flawless models doing this hot trend or that, viewers begin to wonder, *Why can't my life be like that?* Impostor syndrome starts to kick in as they question their abilities and worth.

But what if we defy the stereotype that only young adults are impacted by impostor syndrome resulting from social media? A 2023 study provided by the University of Edinburgh found that reading other people's posts on professional platforms had a significant association with experiencing impostor syndrome when compared to not reading other people's posts. We look at how much money other people make, what degrees they hold, and how successful they are. Self-doubt among many test subjects drove them to address the issue of their *perceived* incompetence by researching and then paying for online skills courses.

Imagine scrolling through your social media feed, seeing colleagues' impressive achievements, and wondering if you truly belong in your professional arena. Everyone on LinkedIn seems to have their act together, making you secretly question your expertise. Sound familiar? That's impostor syndrome at play.

Like the influencers on Instagram and TikTok, our colleagues are posting about the phenomenal work they did on a project, their promotions, or their leap to an amazing job at a new company. I haven't seen many postings about mundane jobs or the project that got screwed up. Have you? What we fail to look at are *our* accomplishments and all that we have achieved. Instead, we look at the filtered posts of others' work, and like the younger generations, we wonder, *Why can't my life be like that?*

"WHAT IF I FAIL?": THE FEAR OF FAILURE

I met Glenn at a master class for speakers. Glenn is a successful pediatric dentist, husband, and father to two precocious little girls. He's one of those people that when he walks in, it's not just his smile but also his whole persona that lights up the room. It's hard not to smile back when you see him.

He also discovered that he is a perfectionist and does not want to put anything out into the world if it contains a possible perception of a flaw. All his life, he has put incredible pressure on himself to be the perfect person, say the right things, show certain emotions, and provide impeccable work. Digging a little deeper, he told me how overly critical he was of himself and that "I never wanted to allow others to poke holes in any part of my life because this would give them a reason not to love me."

His quest for perfection stemmed from childhood trauma and bullying. He said, "It isn't necessarily the fear of failing but the fear of not doing something right." This level of perfectionism and the constant stress to be flawless affected his time in college and in his work, and had started to bleed over into his relationships with his wife and children.

While attending the master course on public speaking and writing his speech, his instructors prodded him to ask the question of why he believed in this concept or that. Not satisfied with the superficial answer, they urged him to look a little deeper into how his belief system took form. Glenn forced himself to start looking into the deep, dark corners of his mind and found three versions of himself: a five- to six-year-old, a ten- to eleven-year-old, and a teenage version. These bullied versions of himself never got to grow up. Instead, they were held in a constant state of unworthiness.

Glenn discovered that success creates value; it doesn't create worth.

Glenn set on a journey to evolve and become a better version of himself for his family. But more importantly, he wants to leave behind perfectionism and the constant need for external validation to be happy. "I've been working to be more kind to not just myself but the versions I've kept inside," he told me as he started to unpack the deep scars from childhood.

Through this work he has had the realization that "the fact is, what we accomplish and what we do are actually not related to our worthiness to be loved."

Glenn discovered that success creates value; it doesn't create worth.

Like Glenn, many perfectionists believe that their merit is tied to the work they produce, how they look, or how they act. They typically have all-or-nothing attitudes. If they can't do whatever it is they set out to do perfectly, it is a failure. It will reflect on them and thus tarnish not just their reputation but also how they see themselves.

The Fears That Drive Us

Atychiphobia, or the fear of failure, is one of the top-ranked fears in the world. Research from the goal-based social network Linkagoal revealed that 49 percent of those polled *admit* that the fear of failure stops them from going after a goal or dream. Forty-nine percent. How many more secretly believe but are unwilling to admit that the fear of failure is stopping them? That percentage is more than the fear of flying (33 percent), fear of spiders (31 percent), fear of public speaking (30 percent), or the fear of a zombie apocalypse (12 percent).

If you run your own company, that fear of failure is even higher. A recent study by Norwest Venture Partners found that 90 percent of CEOs agree that the fear of failure is their main cause of distress.

For years, this was never one of the what-ifs that bothered me. I would get a little zing in my chest when I looked at a hill or a challenge and wonder, *How quickly can I conquer this?* Failure was never an option. I relished being told no or that "you can't do that." These negative, limiting comments just created a more intense fire and drive to succeed.

Sitting in my Engineering 101 course my sophomore year, like a good student, I sat in the middle row, halfway up the stadium seating. Mechanical pencil, check. Lined notebook, check. Excitement to learn what engineers could do, check. But to my left, two boys were snickering. Always up for a good laugh, I asked them what they were laughing about.

One replied, "You can't be an engineer. You're a girl."

Then the other said, "You should go enroll in the business school."

Oh, hell no! They did not just say that! Rage, fury, and a bit of shock shot through my system. It started to dawn on me that engineering would be difficult, but I would also have to deal with the social aspect that came with being a woman working in what many still thought was a man's profession.

My brows knit together as I turned away and ignored them. Right there, on day one of Engineering 101, I vowed to do everything in my power to beat those stupid boys. I would work harder on my homework, do extra credit, and study more fiercely until I knew the course material backward and forward. And I succeeded.

My younger self would always look at a challenge and maybe get a bit jittery. But I would jump in, throwing 100 percent of myself at the problem. It wasn't until years later, when the stakes were higher and maybe I was a bit more mature, that I started to halt at the precipice of making a decision.

In chapter 1, you read about my fear of leaving a cushy job to become an entrepreneur. What I didn't realize at the time was that I was at the Perceive step of the Warrior Framework. It was a real fear. The possibilities of becoming a failure in my husband's eyes and jeopardizing my engineering reputation had me up late at night. *What if I fail?* would ring through my head. Wouldn't you know it? That was the Mean Little Voice spinning its lies, trying to keep me safe by telling me to remain in my comfortable office with no threat of ever failing my family or career.

"WHAT IF I SUCCEED?": THE FEAR OF SUCCESS—IT'S NOT WHAT YOU THINK

To be clear, this is a what-if that I never considered until a few years ago. I wondered, *Is this really a thing*? Even Jerry Seinfeld said, "To me, the whole concept of fear of success is proof that we are definitely scraping the bottom of the fear barrel."

What I didn't realize is that it is more prominent than I had originally thought. The more I dug into it, the more I realized that this might be one of the most malevolent of the three what-ifs. The fear of success isn't saying, "Oh no, I'm successful!" It's much deeper than that. In fact, several clients and colleagues told me that what they thought was a fear of failure was, in truth, the fear of success.

And then I met Anna.

The Monikers of Success and Its Effect on Identity

Two years ago, I was brainstorming ideas for my keynote and exploring the types of fears someone could have: spiders, public speaking, and heights, culminating in the fear of failure. Then my friend Anna asked, "What about the fear of success?"

I just blinked at her for a few seconds before asking, "What?"

As part of my keynote, I speak about one of the remedies for the fear of failure is to move through fear and instead consider: What if you succeed? (We talk more on this in subsequent chapters.) But here was someone standing in front of me. She looks normal, and she talks normal, but she might as well have been an interplanetary alien with green skin and three heads. What she said was so foreign I couldn't wrap my head around it. *Hmm, the fear of success?* I needed to understand this concept, so I asked her to break it down for me.

She relayed a story from her early twenties, after she moved to Boston. "Boston is a running town. It seems like almost everyone there runs. So eventually, I started running with people I met at the gym. We'd sign up for small races and train together." Anna warmed up to the idea of signing up for a full marathon. She got a coach, who provided a rigorous plan. But as the weekly training mileage increased, she began to wonder, *What did I just do?*

During training, she spontaneously decided to try out a friend's triathlon bike. She had an accident that sent her to the hospital. (Her words of wisdom on the accident: Don't clip into a bike and go for a ride in Brookline, Massachusetts, if you have never learned to unclip your feet. It's a bad idea.) Damaging her shoulder to the point of stitches and the need for physical therapy, she could no longer train for the full marathon. Instead, she invited new friends to run it as a relay, each taking three to five miles. She told me that frankly she was "relieved I no longer had to train for the marathon because of my injury." She believes the accident was her inadvertent form of self-sabotage.

I then asked why she signed up for the marathon in the first place. She responded, "I like having goals and something to work toward. Being in a new city, I was lonely and needed a way to spend my time." But what she said next is typical of those with a fear of success: "But it is interesting looking back. I wanted to do that goal, but I didn't believe in myself enough to do the goal, so I sabotaged it."

Soon afterward, a traumatic event in Anna's personal life took running off the table. Depression set in, and after several months, she realized she had reached a low point in her life. That's when she heard about a very unathletic friend signing up for the Duluth Marathon. Hearing this, she vowed, "If he could do a marathon, so can I." This combination of needing a reason to get out of bed each day and a healthy, competitive spirit drove her to sign up for a second marathon. She vowed, "This time, things will be different."

She reenlisted the help of a running coach and was mentally prepared for the long, arduous training process. She followed the training plan to a T and called her coach daily with mileage and time. Each morning, she would put on her running clothes and psych herself up. Before moving to Boston, she had never run more than three miles, and now she was doing mileage that she'd never done before. Anna's mind focused on the length of each weekend training run.

Oh, I'm about to run thirteen miles.
Oh my word. I'm about to run sixteen miles.
Holy smokes! Today I have to run more than twenty miles!

Each time she had to get over a huge psychological hurdle to get out of the house and just do it.

Then two weeks before the marathon, she sat crying in her therapist's office. She remembers telling him, "I don't know. I'm not scared that I can't do it; I'm scared that I can."

I was able to follow her story until that last sentence. I've trained for a marathon and know how grueling it can be, the mental focus that's required, and the strength to just keep running. Leading up to my race, I also got jitters. But for me, that nervousness was the possibility that I would fail and not finish.

For Anna, it was an identity issue. She had never considered herself a runner, let alone a marathon runner. In her mind, running any distance was for elite athletes. She had always told herself, "I'm not a runner or a marathon runner. I'm not capable of these things. Other people are capable of these things. I'm not." She explained the predicament that if she finished the marathon, she would be "a marathoner." That was a moniker saved for other runners, not her. If she finished the marathon, she would have a new way to describe herself. The whole lexicon about who she was and what her identity was would completely shift and be destroyed.

Anna's fear of success was the new identity she would have if she pushed through her fears and came out on the other side.

Anna's fear of success was the new identity she would have if she pushed through her fears and came out on the other side.

The Repercussions of Success

Ashley is a meteorologist whom I recently met while holding a workshop for the US Forest Service. Afterward, she asked if anyone had ever heard of her fear, the fear of success.

Growing up as a Dominican in New York City and Philadelphia, she was raised in a culture where the men were the breadwinners of the family. But her family was different. Having only girls, her father raised her and her sister as if they were sons. Education was of the utmost importance. Her sister is a surgeon, and Ashley has a doctorate and a postdoctorate in meteorology and atmospheric chemistry.

Despite her level of education, Ashley was always at odds with her now former husband, who had a master's degree. She felt like the bar for her dream job and accompanying salary had to be so much higher for him to agree to pick up and move for her. It was more culturally acceptable for her to do that for him. She still thinks about what would have happened if she were able to land that dream job.

With her new partner, she knows she will need to have a hard conversation about relocating to the Pacific Northwest. She wonders, *What if he's intimidated that I will be the main breadwinner for the family? What if he doesn't want to move?* She's considered lowering her expectations and taking a job at her second choice instead of her number-one pick because it avoids the uncomfortable conversations and doesn't change the family dynamics. For Ashley, the fear of success makes her question whether getting her dream job means she must answer hard truths about herself and the security of her relationships. Would her partner move for her? The question is not whether she gets the job but what happens next if she does.

Ashley's fears include what may happen if she gets that dream job and moves up in the hierarchy. Will she be respected in a male-dominated industry? As likely the only woman in the room, she wonders if it is wise to be on a trajectory with men who could view her as being too vocal, too much in the spotlight, and too much of a semipublic figure. As it is, she does what she can to fit in—cargo pants and flannel, no makeup, a braid, and a baseball cap. The job would be the exciting next step up the ladder, but she wonders how much harder others could make her life if she got it. She says, "If it's my uniqueness that I bring to the table that allows me to be successful, there's a fear that it also may be the thing that makes it harder to succeed."

I've talked with clients who fear getting a promotion they deserve because of the ramifications after they step into the new job. They worry that they won't know enough to execute that position. A few clients have told me they initially declined promotions because they didn't want to be a disappointment to their bosses. Would they be smart enough to handle the new responsibilities and be a good leader of a new team, things that often come with a promotion?

As you can already see, there are similarities between the fear of success and impostor syndrome.

> **The main difference is that those with a fear of success are in positions where they feel comfortable, even content, and are looking at that next rung of the ladder.**

The main difference is that those with a fear of success are in positions where they feel comfortable, even content, and are looking at that next rung of the ladder.

They wonder, *If I reach that next rung, what becomes of me?*

Those with impostor syndrome believe they got to their current positions even though they didn't deserve them.

In the worst possible way, it can be circular. Those with a fear of success may push through the fear to reach the goal of a new position, only to wind up feeling out of place and like a fraud once they get there.

> Those with impostor syndrome believe they got to their current positions even though they didn't deserve them.

PROCRASTINATION AND PERFECTIONISM

As seen in Figure 2.2, there is an intersection between the fear of failure and the fear of success.

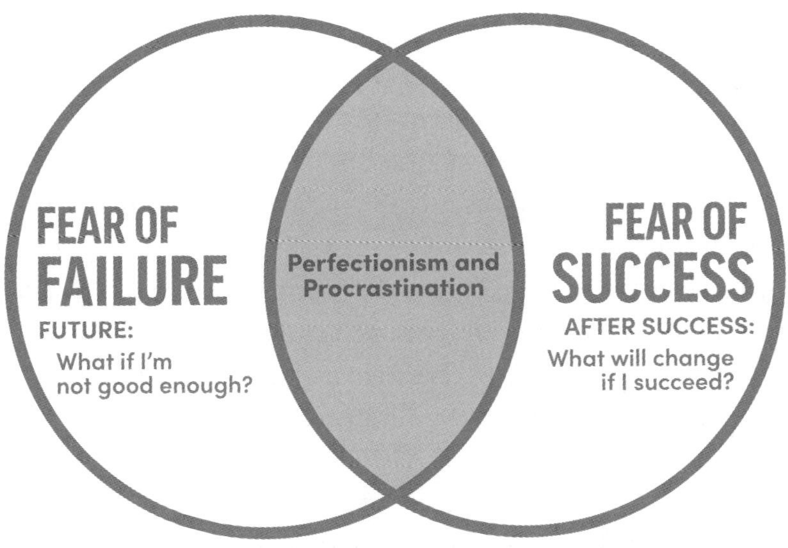

FIGURE 2.2. THE INTERSECTIONALITY BETWEEN THE FEAR OF FAILURE AND THE FEAR OF SUCCESS

Procrastination can manifest in several ways, but its sole purpose is to stop us before we ever get started. The Mean Little

Voice and the Sneaky Little Bastard can tag team each other, just like in a WWE fighting match. The Mean Little Voice will tell you that you will most likely fail. It runs over to the side and taps the Sneaky Little Bastard, who is waiting on the top rope, ready to launch into the ring. The Sneaky Little Bastard's favorite move is procrastination. Because if you procrastinate, you never start, so you will never know the pain of future failure.

Let's be honest. Have you ever spent time looking at Facebook, TikTok, or Instagram instead of sitting down and writing out your plan? It's OK. Don't judge yourself too harshly. There are days when I would rather do my taxes than pick up the phone and call a potential client. I'm afraid I won't be good enough for what they need or will flat out be told no. So my Sneaky Little Bastard helps me find other things to do to keep busy, like cleaning out the dishwasher. The Sneaky Little Bastard has a secondary signature move: perfectionism.

Katie is an engineer. In 2024, she decided to go out on her own and start her own business as a technical writer. After starting my own business several years earlier, I gave her tips for getting up and running. One of those tasks was to get an email out to the community announcing her new company and the direction she was going. Weeks went by. "Katie, it's just a simple email. Don't make it too complicated, but get it out there."

A few more weeks passed. Then she started to tell me all the things she wanted to do before the email went out. The Sneaky Little Bastard had shown up. It told her about all the things she "needed" to do before the email went out. Some were legitimate. But a lot of them weren't. You don't need a logo to send out on the email. It was just another hurdle, tiny though it was, that she put in front of herself to delay sending the email. She rehashed and rewrote the email. It needed to be perfect. She worried about how people would judge her based on the email. What she did not expect was the outpouring of support from the community on her decision to become a business owner.

Perfectionism is shared by the fears of failure and success. Imagine that Sneaky Little Bastard looking over your shoulder saying, “It’s not good enough yet.” We spin our wheels tweaking and may crumple up our drafts and start over. We try to get to 100 percent, but in real life, that goal is unattainable. For the perfectionist, even 99 percent is not good enough. It keeps us from ever taking the next step forward.

PERCEIVING THE COUSINS THROUGH THE WHAT-IFS

I’ve often thought about and had clients ask where the voices come from. If you want to get technical, they come from our prefrontal cortex. This region of the brain creates our sense of self and gives us the ability to reflect on our thoughts and actions. This sense of self essentially gives us an inner voice that guides our behaviors and helps us to navigate complex social environments. In chapter 1, I spoke about instinct and intuition, the foundations that keep us alive and safe. We have learned to listen to them through our own inner monologues developed in the prefrontal cortex, whether we realize that’s what’s happening or not.

The better question to ask is: Why are they sometimes nice and helpful, and why are they sometimes downright mean and everything in between? Scientists believe that the negative thoughts are residue from previous fear-based and self-protective encounters.

Previous failures, dramatic events, or inexperience can cause lower self-esteem and a diminished sense of self.

This reinforces how the Cousins are created to keep you safe by not growing, moving forward, or trying something new.

Previous failures, dramatic events, or inexperience can cause lower self-esteem and a diminished sense of self.

Think of your stream of consciousness as a flowing river. All types of thoughts flow along, just like different types of fish. *I need to add eggs to the grocery list. What will the weather be like tomorrow? I want a raise, but I'm afraid to ask.* Trout, bigmouth bass, carp.

Perceive, step 1, is an active measure to detect and listen to our stream of verbal consciousness. Don't just observe the stream; notice the fish swimming along.

If you are having trouble thinking about your stream of consciousness, I've found the best means is to consider the what-ifs I ask myself. What are the what-ifs in your life? There is a whole library of what-ifs out there. Following are just a few of them:

- What if I'm not smart enough?
- What if I don't make it?
- What if everything I've achieved to this point has been a fluke?
- What if I'm not perfect?
- What if I actually get that job?

I could go on and on. But all the what-ifs are derivatives that fall under the umbrella of impostor syndrome, the fear of failure, and the fear of success.

Let's take the goal on your sticky note, for instance. When you think about that goal, what are the what-ifs that come to mind? An example might be: *What if I'm not ready*?

WARRIOR EXERCISE

What are your major what-ifs?

Now that you are aware of them, it might be easier to sort them and determine where in Figure 2.3 you might land. Which category a what-if is in can vary for individuals. For example, one person may consider her what-if of not being smart enough for the job as a fear of failure, while another considers her same what-if as part of an impostor syndrome. They could both be right.

And here is the most important question to ask yourself: Are your what-ifs rational questions? As we move through the book, I'd like you to give more thought to that question.

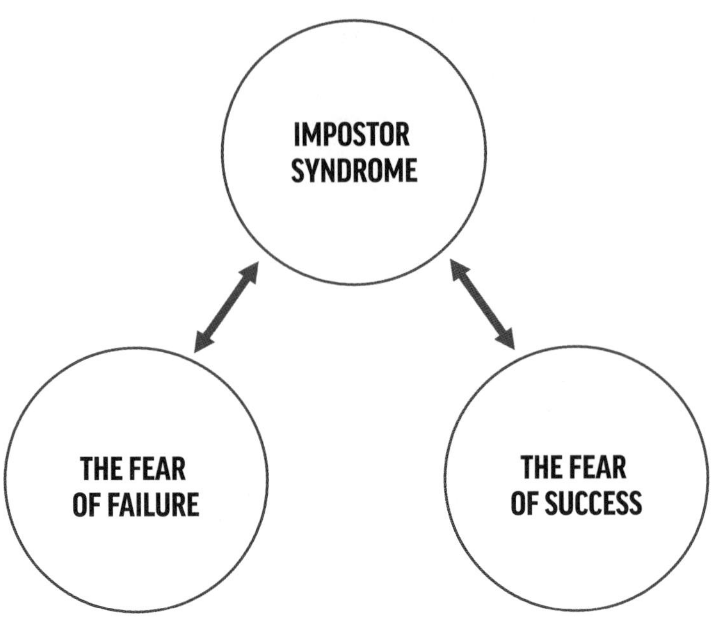

FIGURE 2.3. REVIEW OF THE CONNECTIONS BETWEEN IMPOSTOR SYNDROME, THE FEAR OF FAILURE, AND THE FEAR OF SUCCESS

WARRIOR DEBRIEF

1. Impostor syndrome typically occurs when you feel like you got to your current condition as a fluke or through luck.
2. The fear of failure or success typically occurs when you are looking to grow or try something new, yet the potential outcomes are what you fear most.
3. The best means to initiate the first step of the Warrior Framework, Perceive, is to listen to the what-ifs you ask yourself.

3

ASSESS

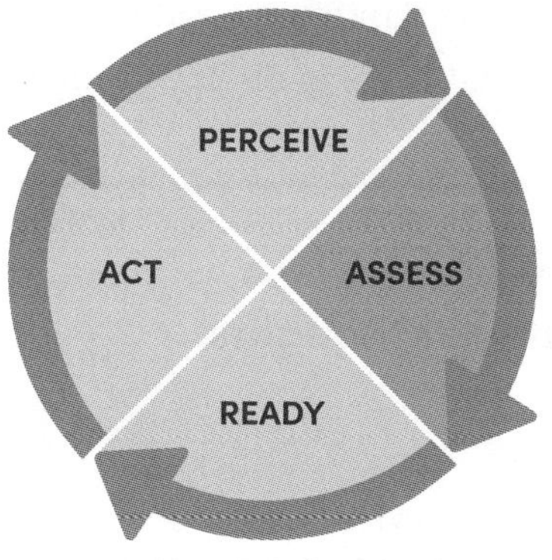

One of my favorite movie series of the late 1990s and early 2000s was *Austin Powers*. It's the swinging 1960s, a time of free love and no-consequence behavior. Having recently defeated his archnemesis Dr. Evil, Austin "Danger" Powers, a part-time playboy and part-time secret agent, agrees to be frozen by the British government in case his services are ever needed again. Of course, his unique set of skills is once more required. Austin is thawed from his cryo-chamber and begins to assess the world around him. He sees his new partner, who is very attractive, and audibly states explicit and ungentlemanly things about her in front of the whole room. While it was possibly more mainstream to say these things in 1967, in 1997, he shocks and disgusts everyone in the room. Seeing the reaction, he realizes his mistake and asks, "How do I let them know because of the unfreezing process, I have no inner monologue?"

We all have thoughts, and many of them we need to keep to ourselves. In the previous chapter, we talked about perceiving the Cousins' voices by recognizing their opening monologues of what-ifs. Now we move to step 2 and Assess which voice is speaking to us. Like the fisherman surveying the river of our stream of consciousness, he is able to see and discern the voices, much like the differences between minnows, salmon, or catfish. It starts with recognizing what is going on in your head.

WARRIOR EXERCISE
Think about your thoughts.

I know this sounds silly, even repetitive and circular.

OK, what just happened there? Did you agree with me? Or did you think, *Hmm, that sounds interesting*? What did you just think when I said, "Think about your thoughts"?

Thinking about your thoughts—or metacognition—is the first step toward self-awareness and being able to harness and control your thoughts.

Many of us have inner monologues. As we explore the world around us, our brain registers and synthesizes the sights, sounds, smells, and textures and then creates comments around them. *What a beautiful sunrise. This is the best hamburger I've eaten in weeks. It's too windy to go for a run today.* Most of us keep our monologues internal.

We also have debates in our head all the time. *Should I have a nice healthy salad when the steak and potatoes look so much more appealing? Should I do this task or that task? Should I run my errand during my lunch break or wait until after work?* This reasoning process is innate, healthy, and an excellent example of the competing thoughts in our heads.

But when negativity begins to enter the process, does the voice sound different? When you are sitting at your desk and need to call a potential client that you have been putting off for whatever reason, does the voice that says, *Maybe we should work on some easy little task*, sound different? Does that voice sound different from the one that says, *Why even call? You know they are just going to say no anyway.*

In chapter 1, we discussed how the Mean Little Voice might sound vastly different from the Sneaky Little Bastard. From that epic breakup with Russell and my mom's terse comments to get over it, I gained an edge in the ability to separate the Mean Little Voice from the everyday, mundane voices. As I said earlier, my Mean Little Voice is easy to detect from its edgy, snide, and mean tone. I can hear its malintent.

But the Sneaky Little Bastard . . . well, it's sneaky for a reason. It still sounds a lot like my normal inner monologue. It's quite easy to listen to for a while before I figure out that it's the Sneaky Little Bastard. Recognizing and assessing the Sneaky Little Bastard is something that I must always stay vigilant about. I have learned to assess whether it is a normal thought process, or the Sneaky Little Bastard by asking myself what I really need to do. Is it calling a client? Is it hitting the word count on my manuscript? Deep down, I know what I need to do. If the choices I've made do not align with that purpose, I know the Sneaky Little Bastard has duped me again, and I need to get myself back on track.

RECOGNIZE THE VOICES? CONGRATULATIONS!

If you have the Mean Little Voice and/or Sneaky Little Bastard, well, congratulations! Why? Let me explain.

Think of a time when you were content. No goals. No dreams. Nothing you wanted to go after. Any voices? Probably not. But it's when you want something that might be outside your comfort zone that they wake up. People who are content and not looking to grow or change rarely hear the Mean Little Voice and Sneaky Little Bastard Cousins. It's when you push yourself that the Cousins wake up. Imagine that they live in a firehouse. When you are content, they are just lounging around, eating Cheetos. When you consider change, that's when the alarms start to go off. They get excited, get suited up, and slide down the fire pole, ready for action.

As I explained earlier in the book, I joined the reserves after active duty. And after working as a civilian for a few years, I used my GI Bill and went back to school for a master's and PhD. Eighteen hours after I turned in my doctoral dissertation, I was reactivated by the navy and sent to Iraq. When I returned, I had a decision to make: (1) Should I start as a full-fledged entrepreneur with my little JL Donahue Engineering, which I began during my graduate work, or (2) Should I go to work for a corporate engineering

> People who are content and not looking to grow or change rarely hear the Mean Little Voice and Sneaky Little Bastard

job? It was the end of 2008, and the United States was in a recession. I had been back on active duty for more than a year and had lost touch with potential would-be clients. In grad school, my company was a hobby and a way to make extra money. Given these reasons, I decided on the second option.

I worked at a great midsize company for six years. I was content. It was a respectable job. I had great clients, incredibly interesting projects, and a nice paycheck. And my life was stable. But as I looked at my entrepreneur colleagues and realized that I, too, could go out on my own, the voices woke up. In the months leading to my resignation, it was like a four-alarm fire was going off in my head. The voices were scrambling around the firehouse, gearing up, and ready to drench my dreams in a barrage of water.

Not having the framework in place yet, I leaned into remembering my mom's words: "Are you going to let them win?"

As an engineer, I am always looking for patterns, designs, causes, and effects. I began to think about why my head was starting to explode with negative thoughts. Finally, it dawned on me: This is something outside my comfort zone. It's something I'd never done before, and it could possibly lead to growth and greatness! It was at this realization that I remember taking a swift inhale as my eyebrows literally shot up! I said to myself, *This is scary. Is this what growth looks like?*

FIND YOUR TRIGGERS

Yes, when I am about to do something outside my comfort zone, the Cousins wake up. It can be a whole host of scenarios, including going into a room where I don't know anyone or entering a boardroom where I might be the youngest or only woman in the room.

I was recently asked to be part of the Navy Seabee Foundation's board of directors. This is a great honor and a way to give back and support the Seabees that I had spent my career with. I was brought in as a representative of the reserves. The board is composed of retired navy admirals (ranks of O7 and O8), captains (O6), and senior enlisted (master chiefs, or E9s). I didn't think too much about it to begin with, but on my small committee, I was working with two admirals and a master chief. While I didn't know the master chief, who I knew served for over thirty years, I had worked for and had huge admiration for both admirals. I started to feel a bit inadequate as only a navy captain, and a reservist on top of that.

In the military, as might be expected, your rank and the ranks of those around you shape how you address each other. There is also an undercurrent of hierarchy for those who retired from active duty compared to reservists.

At my first in-person board meeting, I was the youngest member by quite a bit and the only in-person female officer. Another female officer was attending virtually, but she was former active duty. I was also one of the three newest board members. All these details started to weigh on me. I started to feel like an "only": the *only* female, the *only* reservist, the *only* person in the lower half of my decade, and so on.

The other thirty people were all seasoned board members, mostly type A personalities. All the officers had outranked me while on active duty, and in the reserves, some of them had been my bosses. I sat in my chair, not saying anything. The Mean Little Voice had sealed my mouth shut. *Who would listen to me? What would I have to contribute?*

As the meeting went on, I started to look around, and a realization started to form. *Hey, wait a minute. I'm now the same rank as many of the others in the room. Besides the admirals and enlisted, the rest of us are all navy captains. Yeah, they might have been my bosses ten years ago, but we are on equal footing in retirement.* And there were a few other reservists in the room. I was so wrapped up in my own thoughts and focused on myself that I failed to notice that one was sitting right next to me. I began to see that it didn't make a difference whether you were a captain or an admiral, whether you were formerly active or reserve, because everyone had a voice.

WARRIOR EXERCISE

Stop and think: What are the areas of your life that make you uncomfortable?

____

____

____

I am sensitive to the fact that I retired as a reservist, even though I spent almost eight years on active duty, deployed to two active war zones, and led a battalion and a regiment. I also know that I am sensitive when I'm the youngest woman in the room. Walking into the boardroom gave my Mean Little Voice a playground to run wild. It was going down the slide, navigating the monkey bars, and making itself sick on the merry-go-round.

The Assess step of the Warrior Framework is easier if we understand our triggers. If we know what our triggers are, it's easier to discern who might be doing the talking. For example, I stated that I'm sensitive to being the youngest woman in the room.

If I'm the same age as everyone else, that's OK. It's when I'm the youngest *woman* that I freak out for some reason. Is it rational? No. But at least I know this is one of my triggers. Luckily, getting older is the perfect solution to worrying about being too young.

It's time to look inside again. I asked you to think of the situations in which you are uncomfortable because those are perfect times for the voices to show up. When we get on uneven footing in uncomfortable situations, we become insecure, which creates doubt. Doubts are fuel for the voices. Take notice when the voices start to speak to you.

I also know that I can get insecure about my leadership abilities. Colleagues and troops have told me that I'm one of their favorite leaders, but I just don't get it. I cringe inside because I feel like I'm just doing my job.

During my Afghanistan tour, in addition to dealing with troops dispersed all over the country and a boss who was cruel, there was an assassination attempt on my life. One of our tasks was to train the Afghans to become engineers. As I mentioned earlier in the book, the military needs people who can build bases, repair roads, fix bridges, and so on. For the first few months, after getting everything organized, we were humming right along. Each morning, about thirty of my Seabees and I would circle up next to our ginormous up-armored trucks, review the day's plans one more time, await the interpreter to call, gear up, hop in the trucks, and drive ten miles through the crowded, dangerous streets of Kabul to the Afghan base. We'd spend most of the day there and then return home.

One day the interpreter called and said that the Afghan general didn't want us that day. That was fine. I've had to hold my troops back from time to time based on some last-minute training or an administrative task that might have come down from our higher headquarters.

The second day, the interpreter called and said, "Stand down. The general doesn't want to see you today." OK, now this was getting a little weird.

The Assess step of the Warrior Framework is easier if we understand our triggers.

The third day he called, and I put him on speakerphone. The interpreter stated, "The general is ready to see you again, but make sure your guardian angels are more on point than normal."

That is weird, I thought. *Why would I need my personal security detachment to be more alert than they normally are?* I could already feel a little bit of foreboding.

I asked him, "What's going on?" He calmly answered that insurgents had infiltrated the general's unit and were planning to kidnap me and a few other key players and do horrible things to us before murdering us. But we shouldn't worry. Luckily, the general found out about them through his network of spies and took care of the threat.

According to our interpreter, "You won't have to worry about them anymore. So are you coming out?"

OK, I got it. Getting killed was in the military's job description. But this was somehow different. These were people who knew me by name, and they wanted me dead.

My brain was immediately assaulted by anger, rage, shock, disbelief, and then fear. I knew I had to give the interpreter an answer, but what if I made the wrong decision? I wondered, *What if there were more insurgents out there? What if I go back out there, and they kill me? Or worse, what if they kill some of my people? How would I ever explain to their families that I screwed up and got them killed?*

But what if I decided that we would just stay here today, you know, make sure it was all sorted out? In that case, we would fall behind on our schedule, and every troop around me would think I'm a coward.

Then I heard the Mean Little Voice: *Maybe you are a coward.*

My mind started racing through all the scenarios as I looked around at my people. Some of them looked scared, and some looked angry. Except for the guy way in the back, picking his fingernails so he didn't have to make eye contact.

I had to decide; everyone was looking at me. *A real leader would know what the answer is. A real leader would know exactly what to do.*

Let's step back to realize what an incredibly insane and chaotic situation this is! I might have been killed by insurgents, and the first place my brain goes to is *I'm not a good leader*. I had a life-and-death decision to make, and I let the Mean Little Voice cloud my judgment, preying on my insecurities regarding my leadership ability. I compared myself to all my counterparts. *I bet they would know exactly what to do in this situation and could make a quick decision*. Incidentally, none of my counterparts or any other leaders I was friends with or in contact with who served in Iraq or Afghanistan had ever been in a situation like this.

I let my leadership insecurity open the door for the Mean Little Voice to waltz right in, hands in its pockets, and begin to spew its horrible lies. You may say, "Those voices sound a lot like instinct and intuition." And you would be right. This was a terrifying situation for anyone to be in. Parts of my brain were screaming, *This isn't safe! What am I doing here?*

But the navy, over nineteen years, prepared me to make rational decisions based on the information at hand. Instead of executing the proper thought process of sorting through what I knew, what I didn't know, and what I needed to find out, the Cousins hijacked my brain in a different direction. The Mean Little Voice was telling me I wasn't a good leader. Its wrestling buddy, the Sneaky Little Bastard, was telling me that today would be a perfect day to stay in and do some mundane paperwork.

The noise in my head was incessant. It was so difficult to pick out the input of instinct and intuition and separate them from the Cousins. But finally, the acrid questions seemed to register, and I began to assess that it was the Mean Little Voice. It took me a few more seconds to recognize the Sneaky Little Bastard steering me in a different direction.

We need to understand our insecurities and triggers. They can come in all shapes and sizes, depending on our self-doubts and uncertainties. Do any of these prompts sound familiar?

- I'm the only *X* in the room (*X* is race, gender, or identity), so they won't listen to me.
- Everyone else has years of experience; I have nothing comparable to contribute.
- I don't think people will still love/like me if I go in this direction.
- I don't have the right degrees (master's, MBA, and so on).
- What I am doing is so uncharacteristic and unconventional that others might not accept me.

In the upcoming chapters, we learn how to shore up our defenses.

ANTHROPOMORPHIZING: BIG WORD, BIGGER IMPACT

I've decided to call my Mean Little Voice "Bob." I have nothing against the Roberts and Bobs of the world. It's my favorite uncle's name. And if you are reading this and that is your name, I do apologize. But for me, Bob is an easy name.

WARRIOR EXERCISE

Name one of the voices.

Give it a name, any name. One of my readers called their Mean Little Voice "Negative Echo" because as she explained it, ″NE doesn't just come at me once but echoes the negative sentiment over and over."

Why name the voice? Because we are in the process of personifying that voice. It is a part of you, yet you have the power to segregate your thoughts. The process of naming our voices and feelings has existed for thousands of years. It's called anthropomorphizing. Big word, but it basically means we assign human characteristics or traits to inanimate objects, animals, or thoughts.

We place human emotions on things like toasters, computers, pets, or cars. Let's consider your car. Have you ever named it? I once had an old gray beater Toyota Corolla that I used as a commuter car. I called it "Zippy." It was a fitting name. It wasn't flashy; it wasn't even fast. When I looked at Zippy, it always seemed to be smiling. And when I drove him, it felt like he had a fun demeanor, like he wanted to say, "Hey, let's go for an adventure." OK, I get it. It's a car. Cars are not male or female, and they don't have demeanors or look for adventures. Yet we anthropomorphize objects around us more than you may realize. My husband swears his iPhone has a personality disorder.

When it comes to emotions, our ancestors had anthropomorphism down to a science! They created deities that represented love, wisdom, beauty, and power. They also created deities that represented our weaknesses, such as mischief, greed, hatred, jealousy, and anger. For example, let's take mischief. Many cultures have their god of mischief: Eris (Greek), Loki (Norse), the Monkey King (Chinese), Wisakedjak (Navajo), and Anansi (West Africa). As explained by the philosopher David Hume, "Humans anthropomorphize to explain the mysteries of life and the world around us." We use what we know: our human selves and our emotions. We model objects, pets, iPhones, and deities after human traits.

The Pixar movies *Inside Out* and *Inside Out 2* provide perfect examples of anthropomorphizing. The first movie introduces the emotions of a ten-year-old girl, Riley: Joy, Anger, Fear, Disgust, and Sadness. The emotions are individuals working together to help her cope with the challenges of moving from Minnesota to San Francisco. Each emotion participates as she navigates leaving her friends and going into the unknown. In the second movie, the little girl has started to grow up and hits puberty, and her new emotions—Anxiety, Envy, Embarrassment, and Boredom (or Ennui)—make their entrances.

The movies are not just some fanciful ideas by the geniuses at Pixar. Rather, they were developed from research by Dr. Paul Ekman and Dr. Dacher Keltner. Their research on emotions found that there are universal emotions that all humans feel that transcend language and regional, cultural, and ethnic differences.

Psychology has used personifying our feelings for several decades. Anthropomorphism can make it easier to talk about feelings from a safe emotional distance.

Why this lengthy discussion on anthropomorphism? I want you to see that it's not weird to consider the voices in your mind as individuals. It's rather commonplace and can be productive.

Getting back to Bob. By naming this voice, I've found it has become easier to call it out amid the other voices. *OK, Bob is at it again. Bob's running his mouth. Shut up, Bob.* There is something satisfying when once you perceive the voice and then assess that it is not instinct, not intuition, but a nefarious voice to call it out and shut it down.

> There are universal emotions that all humans feel that transcend language and regional, cultural, and ethnic differences.

IT'S TIME TO DECIDE

Have you recently been in a meeting and were afraid to voice your opinion because you didn't think it was that good? Have you looked at a job listing and thought, *I'm not ready yet* or *I'm not good enough*?

WARRIOR EXERCISE

Stop and think: What recent events have triggered the Mean Little Voice or the Sneaky Little Bastard?

____

____

____

Here's the heavy question: What do you wish the outcome had been like? Did you have a great idea and wished you could have contributed? Did you know deep down that you were ready for that job?

I want you to grab a piece of paper again. Go ahead. I'll wait for you.

Write down a scenario when either the Mean Little Voice or the Sneaky Little Bastard stopped you or made you pause and doubt yourself. Maybe it's something relatively small and mundane, like speaking up in a meeting. Maybe it is a life-changing situation, like going after a new job. Just write it down.

Look at that paper and decide whether you are going to allow the Cousins to continue to win. If the answer is no, and I hope it is, destroy that paper. Scribble all over it. Crumple it up. Set it on fire. Use it to pick up your dog's poop. I don't care. The more creative, the more the idea will stick with you.

Realize that the voices have stopped you from achieving your goal thus far. And if you continue to let them in and run around like wild beasts, they will continue to hold you back.

GET A BATTLE BUDDY

I hope you had fun destroying your paper. Doing a physical activity such as destroying paper has a way of waking one's brain and telling you that you are acting and moving forward.

Ready for your next adventure? I have one more activity for you in this chapter. I want you to find a Battle Buddy.

WARRIOR EXERCISE

Who will be your Battle Buddy?

____

____

____

In the military, you have a Battle Buddy, and you go everywhere together. It doesn't matter whether it was in a war zone or back home. This person will always have your back. Your Battle Buddy always knows where you are because he or she is always with you—even when you go to the bathroom. (Which was awkward since I was typically the only female officer, so my Battle Buddy was a dude.)

YOUR HOMEWORK

1. Find a Battle Buddy. This might be a close friend, a member of the family, or a colleague. This is someone you trust, someone you will be answerable to as you decide to move forward.
2. Ask the person to be your Battle Buddy. Explain that a Battle Buddy keeps another person accountable for an upcoming project.
3. (Optional) If you are ready, explain the sticky note you created in chapter 1.

In future chapters, we engage more with your Battle Buddy. Don't worry if you can't name your Battle Buddy at this moment. I've had a few readers struggle with finding the right one. A Battle

Buddy is not the golden ticket to continue to chapter 4. Put it on your to-do list, and let the search begin.

This is part of your journey. All great heroes had a sidekick. Sherlock had Dr. Watson, the Lone Ranger had Tonto, and Frodo had Samwise. Even solitary, brooding Batman had Robin and Alfred. You are becoming the hero, or warrior, of your life. But I warn you there is a possibility that one of two things will happen when you pick a Battle Buddy.

One, they will be superexcited for you. This is probably someone who has known you for a long time and is excited that you are moving in a different direction. This person may become your biggest cheerleader.

Two, they may derail you. Let's face it. You have many obligations in your life. If this new venture is going to cause instability, your Battle Buddy might try to talk you out of it or tell you to delay it until a later time. There may also be the case that your Battle Buddy might become jealous. They will see you moving forward, progressing toward your goal, and leaving them behind. If this is the case, find a new Battle Buddy.

You will encounter naysayers along your journey. It's not just the Sneaky Little Bastards in our heads that tell us to delay. It might be friends or family. I'll help you deal with the naysayers in chapter 7.

WARRIOR DEBRIEF

1. Once we learn to perceive the many voices in our head, it's time to assess whether they are friend or foe. The Assess step investigates different ways to evaluate if the voices are rational or just a series of made-up scenarios.
2. Understand what might trigger the voices.
3. Anthropomorphizing is a constructive means to separate the Mean Little Voice and the Sneaky Little Bastard from other rational voices.
4. Celebrate if you have the voices roaming around in your head. This means you are trying something new, something outside your comfort zone. You are growing.

4

INTRODUCING THE WARRIOR: READY, PART 1

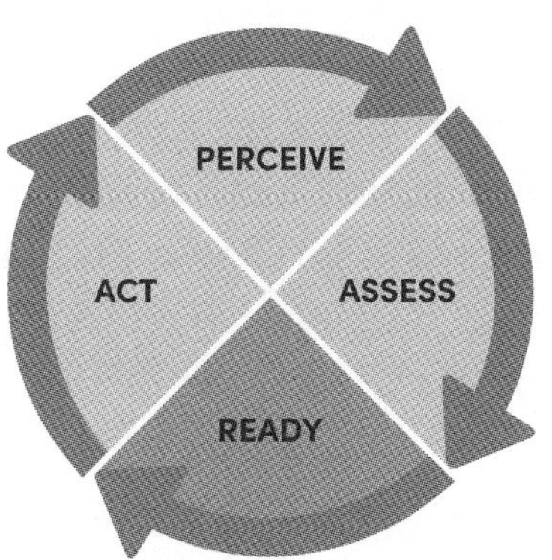

The Euphrates River is famous for straddling the cradle of civilization with its sister river, the Tigris. Near the tiny village of Baghdadi, upriver and northwest of Baghdad, the vegetation along this stretch was composed mainly of tall reeds. Yet fifty yards from the riverbank stretched endless miles of light tan sand. Children tended to flocks of fluffy sheep. It was still mid-March, so the temperatures were mild, if not a bit cold overnight.

I assigned Don to be the officer-in-charge of a team of thirty Seabees to build the world's second-longest float bridge upstream from the town. It was 2008, and this quadrant in Iraq, Al Anbar Province, was well known for insurgent ratlines—established routes for insurgents from Syria to provide fighters, weapons, and explosives to the opposition. The float bridge would provide easy access for Iraqi and coalition units to traverse. The only options currently available were circling up to Haditha Dam or driving all the way down to Baghdad to cross. This bridge would cut their travel time by about six hours.

Don had only been in Iraq for two weeks. A navy reservist from Northern California, his civilian job was as a senior superintendent on major construction projects. In one of his jobs, he oversaw the building of a nine-story complex in downtown San Francisco. With no area to lay down material or equipment, he ran such a tight schedule that the tower crane was booked in five-minute increments. Don knows how to build and get things done. Yet San Francisco was a long way from the deserts of Iraq.

From the start of the project, there were a few issues. The biggest hiccup was that the US Marines were originally coordinated to provide security for his team. The idea was that they would keep watch for insurgents while Don's team got to work on creating the accessway for the bridge. The problem was that the marines were stretched thin in Al Anbar Province and could only provide about eight people.

"Oh crap! That's not enough," Don said to himself.

As it grew late on the day they arrived, Don realized he needed to make sure his people were safe. They promptly set up their tents and then used their bulldozers to create large earthen berms around them. This would keep his people from being seen by possible bad guys and stop any stray bullets that might come their way during the night. They used only the weapons they all had and rotated people through periods of being on watch and sleeping.

Sleep eluded Don that night, and he bolted upright as he heard strange noises. When dawn broke, Don found one of the marine sergeants and promptly asked, “What the hell was that last night? Why were you guys making those noises?”

“Oh, no sir. That wasn’t us. Those were the feral dogs. They make noises like humans. They’re vicious, and you have every right to shoot them. Just don’t shoot one of your people. So be on the lookout.”

“Double crap! First insurgents, and now feral dogs that attack humans,” was all Don could say.

Don worked with the marines over the next several days to provide a safe area for his team to work, eat, and sleep. They strung concertina wire—razor-sharp wire that makes barbed wire look tame—around the camp for added security. He set up a rotation where there was always someone on the radio and on watch. Construction of the boat ramp and accessway continued without any major problems.

His team worked with incredible efficiency. Each day there was a dance of dozers, excavators, and dump trucks. Sitting on a bluff observing the interplay of the machinery, Don took his turn as the overwatch for security. They were situated at a bend in the river, so everything downstream was in a veritable blind spot that always had to be monitored. As he watched the loading operations, he saw something downriver out of the corner of his eye. A Toyota Hilux came barreling down the road toward their camp. The hairs on the back of his neck began to rise. The locals knew they were there, and whoever this was definitely didn’t.

The Hilux driver saw the concertina wire at the last second and skidded to a halt. Two men bolted from the vehicle and went prone in the tall grass and wheat field.

Goose bumps rising on Don's arms, he dropped to a knee, took his weapon off safe, and immediately began giving commands for his team to stop and take cover. "Oh shit." Without a pair of binoculars or a scope on his rifle, it was hard to tell if they were good guys or bad. If they were the latter and had weapons with scopes, he was exposed and would soon be dead. Don sprinted to a nearby excavator and hid behind the tracks. But he was still able to keep the two men in sight. And he waited and waited and waited.

Time slowed to what felt like an eternity. Where was the quick reaction force of extra marines? Don got up again and sprinted to the other set of tracks to get a better angle. Still, he watched, unable to engage.

The rules of engagement in Iraq at the time required that you could not shoot unless your life or another's life was in danger. But you also must have gotten a positive identification of who's shooting at you before you return fire. It put you in a very precarious position. So here were these two guys. They could have been two teenagers just messing around or someone looking for a fight. There was no way to tell. If he took a preemptive shot, he could go to jail. But at the same time, he also hoped he didn't end up dying right then and there.

Unfortunately, the excavator driver didn't have a radio, so once again, Don sprinted in the opposite direction to find the marines.

"Follow me," he yelled at a group of marines upstream.

They circled back toward the excavator, the concertina wire, and the waiting Hilux. But by the time they got there, only the impressions of two bodies remained in the grass.

I later asked Don about his thought process of going from

seeing the potential threat to smoothly bringing up his weapon, clicking off the safety, taking a knee, and aiming, yet not firing until he had positive identification. Was it instinct or training? He told me it was instinct based on previous training at another unit. He had previously worked with Naval Special Warfare, the SEALs, and spent a couple of hundred hours practicing those procedures and training on different simulations and scenarios. "It was instantaneous." It wasn't about training step 1, do this, and then training step 2, do that, and so on. It had become one fluid motion, instinct created from training.

Until I was a broken-down mess after returning from Afghanistan, with bad bosses, grievances to deal with, and my Seabee's suicide, I never needed step 3 of the Warrior Framework: Ready. Steps 1 and 2 were easy; I could recognize the Mean Little Voice and turn it off. Voices came up, and I shut them down. Voices came up again, and I shut them down again. Shampoo, rinse, repeat.

I let the voices passively come and go. I never thought about the deeper meaning for why the voices were coming in the first place. I did not consider any triggers that would bring them running in like they had heard the dinner bell. While unfortunately I let myself sink to rock bottom, in a way, I am grateful. It forced me to look at what was going on in my head and my life.

I never thought about the deeper meaning for why the voices were coming in the first place.

Ready is an active step. It's more than shutting down and ignoring the voices. It's about taking measures to protect yourself from the voices. To do this, you need a counterpoint.

ORIGIN OF THE WARRIOR

One of my favorite songs as a kid was "Holding Out for a Hero," by Bonnie Tyler. I'd throw on my Walkman, grab the hairbrush, and sing and dance like no one was watching. If you are not a great singer, the key is to crank up the Walkman until you can't hear your own voice. One line in the chorus describes the hero as someone strong, fast, and who has successfully completed a fight.

There was always something about that line that I loved. I imagined this huge, muscled dude striding off the battlefield, victory in his wake, ready to sweep me off to some unknown land. There are tons of similar lines in the song, but that one always stuck with me. It was the mental manifestation of a hero to me. A warrior.

I always wondered when I would meet my hero. Throughout grade school and high school, he never showed up. No sweaty, sooty, sword-wielding, six-foot-five-inch guy ever came and knocked on my door. I grew tired of waiting.

What I am about to say now might shatter whatever image you have of me. I'll just come out and say it: I'm a nerd. I've always loved science fiction and comic book heroes. *Star Wars* is and will always be my favorite movie. Instead of gravitating toward Barbie, I was more into the *ThunderCats* and *X-Men*. Never wanting to be the damsel in distress, I loved the idea of being a blaster-wielding, sword-carrying badass out to save the world.

Instead of waiting around for a hero, what would it be like if *I* became a hero? What if I became a warrior in my own life and helped others? Could I ever become brave enough to look something evil or sinister in the eye, shoulders squared, glare back, and say, "Not today"?

Becoming a hero would be a bit of a tall order, especially since I am naturally a shy introvert. But I imagined starting to stand up for myself and speak when it was my turn. It all sounded good in my head, but it never materialized when I wanted it to.

What I hadn't realized yet was that there is a warrior living inside me. In addition to the instinct, intuition, Mean Little Voice, and Sneaky Little Bastard, there is a voice of strength. I just didn't know how to wake it up when I needed it.

In the previous chapters, we began to develop an awareness to perceive instinct, intuition, and the Cousins. As the next step, Assess, we learned to distinguish each voice and even personified our Mean Little Voices and the Sneaky Little Bastards by giving them names. Now it's time to find your Warrior.

Yes, you have a warrior living within you, whether you realize it or not. Like the Cousins, your Warrior has evolved out of instinct and intuition. In chapter 1, you wrote down a goal or dream. Where did that idea come from? It had to come from somewhere.

Did you hear a little voice say, "I think I can do this"? Is your goal something that you have always wanted to do or something that someone mentioned and sounded like a good idea. A part of your brain connected a few neural pathways to produce that goal. There is a part of your brain that wants you to succeed. Your Warrior lives in that space.

Once I was able to perceive and assess the part of my brain that was trying to derail me, I could block it out and concentrate on what I was trying to do. For instance, I dreamed of trying out for the swimming team, becoming an engineer, and traveling the world. Whatever the goal or dream was, I started to listen for a little voice that said, *I can*, or *I really want this.*

Michelle, the pilot from chapter 2, had a little voice that said, *I'm exhausted. I can't do this anymore. I need a change.* For a pilot on a collision course in her life, where one slip-up could mean catastrophic effects, Michelle was smart enough to listen to that voice. She knew she could no longer let the Mean Little Voice rule her decisions and actions. The voice that said, *This is enough! You can't go on like this; you need to find another way*, was the awakening of her Warrior.

Glenn, the dentist, admits that he has a conversation with his three younger selves, but the voice he chooses is the forty-five-year-old version of himself. This rendition now has all the space, time, and love of an older brother he always wanted to take care of him. The forty-five-year-old Glenn tells the younger Glenns that "they will grow up to do amazing things and add value to this world. They don't have to worry about proving their worth, but simply accept that they are worthy and have a wonderful, beautiful, amazing partner and children into which they can invest."

For Anna, the marathoner, she wanted to achieve her goals. She would not have signed up for a marathon, of all things, if she didn't want to achieve it. She could have easily signed up for a 5K race. But deep in her mind, the Warrior was stirring, urging her to go after something great.

For the run-of-the-mill impostor syndrome or self-doubt that crept in, it was easy to recognize and shut down the Mean Little Voice using my mother's mantra. But when the stakes were high and the stress too intense, there was a cacophony of yelling and chaos going on in my head. My mother's mantra no longer worked because I had come to believe all the lies the Cousins told me.

Trying to find a way to put myself back together, I remembered that tiny voice, the one that said, *I can*. If I had a Mean Little Voice and a Sneaky Little Bastard, who was this tiny voice that wanted to be heard?

That's the voice I yearned to hear and listen to again. It was the voice of quiet confidence. It was the voice that urged me to join the navy in the first place, so I could go out and see the world. It was the voice that sought adventure and experiences. Moving forward, I knew I needed something stronger than just a mantra. I needed a counterpoint to those malevolent voices. It needed to be stronger and with a volume so loud it could overwhelm the Cousins.

I named it Warrior. It wasn't a warrior at that time. It was weak and flimsy, and could be easily trampled. Falling back on my somewhat athletic days in high school and college, I realized that to become stronger, you needed to train. So why not try to train my brain?

IT'S ALL ABOUT MINDSET

There are many types of mindsets. You have probably heard or read about positive and negative mindsets. There are also books on various aspects of mindsets, such as a Reset Mindset (Penny Zenker), Greatness Mindset (Lewis Howes), Wealth Mindset (Arash Vossoughi), and Success Mindset (Ryan Gottfredson). All these mindsets fall under the umbrella of the master mindsets: fixed and growth.

Mindsets are a hot topic in research today. Dr. Carol Dweck of Stanford University provides a clear example of a fixed and growth mindset: "In a fixed mindset students believe their basic abilities, their intelligence, their talents, are just fixed traits. In a growth mindset students understand that their talents and abilities can be developed through effort, good teaching, and persistence."

Those with a fixed mindset believe that they cannot grow or develop further. They believe they are old dogs that can't learn new tricks. I'm guessing that if you are reading this book, you do not fall into this camp.

Those with a growth mindset believe they can improve, get smarter, and become more successful, creative, productive, or positive by working at it.

The Warrior Mindset clearly falls into the growth mindset

> Your mind can be developed, but it takes training and determination.

column. Your mind can be developed, but it takes training and determination. It comes from a will to want or need a change so badly that you will work hard to learn a way to change your current way of thinking.

THE MAKINGS OF THE WARRIOR MINDSET

You may be wondering, *Why Warrior? Why not just give it another name, like Winning Mindset or Badass Mindset?* Let me ask you: What image comes to mind when you hear "warrior"? When I've asked people what a warrior is to them, I get a wide range of ideas, like He-Man, Navy SEALs, samurai, and Amazons (the women warriors, not the website).

A warrior is more than being a winner or a badass. Will they win the battle? Sure. Do they look like badasses? Absolutely. But being a warrior is deeper and more holistic than those other descriptors. A warrior has both strength and mental toughness. The impression of a warrior is someone with courage, focus, and perseverance.

Let's be clear about what a Warrior Mindset is not. It is not about putting on a suit of armor, grabbing a sword, and slaying anyone who stands in your way. Folks, that's murder. That's not what I am advocating. I'm also not asking you to start looking like a warrior. You don't need to head out to the gym and start pumping iron. And for goodness' sake, don't start wearing a loincloth. We are developing our metaphysical warriors.

Warriors throughout history came from a wide range of diverse cultures and backgrounds. Some were trained slaves, while others were nobility. Yet when I compare various warriors through time, I've found four traits that are the most pertinent to a Warrior Mindset. Let's break them down.

Discipline

Discipline is the foundation of a warrior's life. Discipline is about having self-control and staying focused on your goals, even with distractions or temptations. Even the evil Cousins. A warrior's discipline is rooted in an unwavering determination and mental fortitude.

The Warrior Mindset is a conscious decision not to let the voices win anymore. It's about committing to overcome your obstacles through the consistency of a new thought pattern.

In the military, we talk about discipline in every aspect of our lives. It's why we wake up at ungodly hours in the morning. We march in strict formations, each movement coordinated with those around us. We respect the ranks of others and follow orders. We place the good of the unit above our needs.

Discipline is standing in pumps in a military formation for ninety minutes, rigid as a statue, while your toes smash against the front of your shoe, the balls of your feet fill with blood, and you lose the feeling in your legs. You stare straight ahead unflinchingly, not squinting despite the sun beaming in your face. I realize this is a silly statement about the dangers of wearing pumps to a long ceremony, but it also provides insight into discipline. The mind is strong and can bend the will of the body. To ensure the formation remained perfect, I couldn't wiggle, stretch, or even blink too long. The mind is stronger than the circumstances around you.

A lifelong friend, Paul, is a Juilliard-trained musician and holds black belts in Juijitsu and Aikido and the rank of Guro in the Villabrille-Largusa

The mind is strong and can bend the will of the body.

Kali system. He is also a certified StrongFirst level II Kettlebell instructor. He's pretty much a total badass and the most disciplined person I know. When I asked him what discipline means, he replied, "To me, it means extraordinary self-control, and it has enabled me to fully embrace all the different avenues I choose to express myself with." It all started with his music background. As a child, Paul spent countless hours each day with his trumpet and took this discipline to the practice rooms of the conservatory. But when you take it to the extent that Paul did, he says, "What you spend a consistent amount of time with eventually just becomes part of you. Consistency comes from discipline, and you start to get closer and closer to excellence."

Developing discipline begins with knowing your why. Everyone's reason for going after a goal or dream will be different. But no matter what yours is, you must have a strong why as your driving motivation. And as one of my clients told me, "I just wanna," in the end, didn't cut it. When considering your why, you may have to revert to your two-year-old self and repeatedly ask why. Let's say that my goal is to lose weight. Why? So my clothes will fit better. Why? Because I broke my leg a year ago, let myself go, and gained a bunch of weight. Why? Because I was feeling sorry for myself. Why? Because I don't feel sorry for myself anymore and know that I need to have a healthier outlook on life. Why? Because I want to reduce my risk of health issues. Why? Because I want to live a long life with my husband. I could keep going, but that right there is a pretty good why.

Go back to your sticky note from chapter 1 and consider why you want to go in that direction. If you don't have your why completely nailed down now, don't worry. We will go deeper into your why in the next chapter. You may even find that you can modify or refine it as we go along.

WARRIOR EXERCISE

What is your why?

____

____

____

If you don't have a strong why, your heart will not be into the matter, and the whole journey becomes mechanical. It's much easier to develop discipline when it involves something you want to do. And there will be times when you have unpleasant tasks. But discipline helps you to do the stuff you don't like to do.

Paul has translated the discipline he learned at Juilliard into the other aspects of his life. A new goal, a new why, a new routine. Paul told me about teaching others in martial arts: "Many new students get discouraged after a short while when they realize they won't become Bruce Lee in two weeks." Paul has dedicated countless hours to footwork, punches, strikes, blocks, strength training, and endurance. Not every session was fun. It took discipline to keep going back and training through all the pain and soreness. "You have to embrace it all for it to become a part of you." He learned he could make the unpleasant training sessions more pleasant if he concentrated on his purpose.

How do you develop discipline? Start small. To develop the habit of consistency and discipline, you need to commit to a small, manageable task every day. Notice I said *small*. No more than five minutes. Here is an example. My most recent goal was to author this book. Why? I know in my heart that I

To develop the habit of consistency and discipline, you need to commit to a small, manageable task every day.

have a lot to share, and this could be the vehicle to help others with their hurdles. It's a means of making the world a better place. My one small step to discipline was spending five minutes a day for a few months writing down stories and teaching points, thinking about whom I would interview, and conducting research. As you already read, I'm not a huge fan of writing. I would set the timer of my phone to five minutes and then concentrate on this one task. I found that as weeks went by, I often ignored the timer and kept going. It was starting to become not only tolerable but also fun as I started to see all the possibilities. I discuss more about discipline and small tasks at the end of the chapter.

To help maintain discipline, Paul surrounded himself with people who were also on the quest for excellence. "At the conservatory, everyone was on the same page and very competitive." Jokingly, he told me in his Boston accent, "If you've got a bunch of knuckleheads around you, they are not going to support you in your goal." While I can't vouch for the number of knuckleheads around you, this is where your Battle Buddy comes in. Your Battle Buddy is the one to encourage you and keep you on task. If you don't have a Battle Buddy yet, consider talking to a mentor or a teacher. Be selective and surround yourself with people who know what and how you want to achieve your goal.

Resilience

A warrior's resilience is reflected in the capacity to recover from setbacks. Whether it's a defeat in battle or a personal loss, a resilient warrior learns from these experiences and uses them as stepping stones for future success. Failure is a part of the journey, and it's what you do after failure that defines you. True strength lies in the ability to rise after falling. We will learn more about recovering from failures and pitfalls in chapter 7.

Resiliency is fueled by your deep sense of purpose or commitment to a cause—in other words, your why. Let's go back to that sticky note on your desk. Your brain would not have developed that thought if you knew deep down that you couldn't do it eventually. Your why is the fuel that provides the motivation to keep pushing forward despite the hardships and setbacks you will encounter.

Greg, a dear friend of mine, was born with a congenital heart condition. At one week old, he had his first surgery and was not expected to live past three years old. Miraculously, when Greg was six and in the hospital again, his father made a point for Greg to stop letting the doctors come and go without giving him any explanation. His father laid out the harsh reality. He told him that this was not his problem or his mother's. It was Greg's, and he would have to live with and take control of it for the rest of his life, however long that might be. Greg needed to understand what was wrong with him, what people were doing, why they were doing it, and whether it was something he wanted done to him. They were his choices and not for anyone else to make.

It was in that hospital bed, at that young age, that Greg had to take a long, hard look at how he wanted to live his life and what he wanted to do. He made it past age six, and when he asked what his life expectancy would be, the doctors just answered, "Every day is a blessing." Greg was told he wouldn't graduate from high school or be able to drive a car. He has now had more than thirty surgeries, eight of which required cracking his chest open, and a heart transplant.

Instead of looking at his situation as a curse, he took a much different approach. He's a fighter. His internal dialogue was to completely resist when someone told him he wouldn't be able to do something. "I don't care. I'm going to do it anyway." And there often were a few expletives in there as well.

Greg told me about being encouraged to attend a meeting for people with congenital heart conditions. But he couldn't relate to the others. They all felt sorry for themselves and wanted to stay in their houses, basically encapsulated in bubble wrap. He wants to experience life and explore. Today he snowboards, travels extensively, and has a beautiful wife and two adult sons.

Greg still goes in regularly for blood work and has had minor surgeries since his transplant. There have also been a few serious scares, hospitalizations, and setbacks. It would be so easy for him to give up, but his resilience is fueled by his why: the drive to experience the world and to be a good husband and father. And for those reasons, he will continue to pick himself up from whatever obstruction he experiences and fight on.

Trained

Warriors train rigorously, honing their skills and preparing themselves for the unpredictable battle. This preparation helps them to remain focused and composed under pressure, allowing them to adapt to changing circumstances and continue fighting, even when the odds are against them.

One of the main reasons we train in the military is to be ready for the unexpected. Each year, our battalion would gear up and go out on a field training exercise at Fort Hunter Liggett. This hilly section of central California is brutally hot in the summer and freezes during the winter. Spring and fall aren't that much better, especially when you are sleeping in a one-person pup tent and each meal is a prepackaged meal ready to eat (MRE).

The point of a field exercise was to simulate what would happen if you needed to deploy to a hostile region. We would run through a series of drills of things that might be expected. The instructors would start with small scenarios. They would make sure we knew the basics and were able to sort out each situation. Each day, the scenarios would get a little harder by incorporating new wrinkles into the lessons learned on previous days. They would also throw them at us all hours of the day and night to keep us on our toes. By the end of the second week, it felt like they were throwing the kitchen sink at us. They even went so far on the last day as to "kill off" a few of the highest-ranking people in the battalion to make sure that everyone knew how to step up and still accomplish the mission. We always had a plan going into the field exercise, but in those two weeks, when everyone was subjected to the elements, a lack of sleep, and ever-changing circumstances, it became a crucible of how well trained our people were under constant pressure.

Training can be incorporated into every aspect of our lives. It involves doing the same thing repeatedly to build strength or create muscle memory. Let's take playing the piano. I took lessons when I was twelve and practiced for a half hour every day. First, a warm-up with the scales. I then went on to whatever music piece my teacher provided. With practice, after a year I wasn't half bad, but I haven't touched a piano since I was thirteen. I'd be lucky to remember how to play "Chopsticks." The same can be said for learning a different language or starting a training routine to run a marathon. To become proficient, you must consistently train several times a week for a specified period. Each day it becomes a little easier. As you learn a language, you create new neural pathways that expand and strengthen. If you are training for a marathon, the muscles of your legs, your core, and your lungs morph and get stronger. But in both cases, if you stop practicing, the memory and muscles start to fade.

I was recently made aware of the term "monkey mind." This originates from Buddhist principles that refer to a state of being unsettled, restless, or confused. The monkey mind refers to our constantly thinking minds, swinging wildly from one thought to another without purpose. We've all been there. The Buddhist remedy to calm this state is through mindfulness practices to control the mind.

Tammy is a retired US Air Force pilot and an advocate for mental performance training. When I asked her how she trains her brain, she used the example of meditation. Intellectually, she understood that it makes sense and that there was science behind it. Her biggest resistance to meditation was the worry that she would never be able to shut her mind off. What she didn't understand is that it's not about shutting your mind off. Rather, it's about controlling your mind. Her mentor told her, "If your mind wanders away from your focus point and you gently bring it back without judgment, that's meditating. You're in control of your mind. But if your thoughts wander away to your grocery list, your to-dos, or other distractions, and you don't return to your focus point, you've stepped out of meditation."

The monkey mind refers to our constantly thinking minds, swinging wildly from one thought to another without purpose.

Through meditation, Tammy has learned how to

control her focus and breathing when it counts. As she explained, "When you are in an aircraft going a couple of hundred miles per hour and something goes wrong, it's not like you can just pull over on a cloud. You must be in control of your mind to sort out what needs to be done in that instance."

A Warrior Mindset also needs to be trained. We can actively rewire our brain if we have a regime that creates bonds and neural pathways, and we continually strengthen them. The author Idowu Koyenikan states, "The mind is just like a muscle—the more you exercise it, the stronger it gets and the more it can expand." Throughout this book, I have provided exercises to get you started on this path. It's up to you to continue them.

Prepared

The discipline, resilience, and training physically and mentally ensure that warriors are always prepared. Proficiency in all three creates focus, which allows them to be more adaptable and ready to make quick decisions in unpredictable situations. Warriors do not go looking for a fight but know the battleground and are ready to defend it.

The Warrior Mindset is an active, not a reactive, mindset. It is alert and at the ready. Here is what I mean. For many self-help programs, the focus is on defeating impostor syndrome, self-doubt, or fear after it has taken hold. This is reactive. The Cousins are undeterred, and there is an open door to come in when they choose, to waltz around and create havoc.

Alternatively, your Warrior knows its turf. An active Warrior Mindset will not let the Cousins invade and gain a foothold. While we may never be able to fully stop them from materializing and attempting to infiltrate the mind, we can stop them before they do any harm.

The battlefield of your mind is always evolving.

The battlefield of your mind is always evolving. Consider your triggers and any challenges you see on the horizon. You might have an exceedingly difficult day coming up with a meeting that you have been dreading. Maybe there is a task that feels insurmountable but has been outstanding for a while and must now be dealt with. An open tryout may finally become available for a team that you've been wanting to play for. Whatever your goal, be prepared to accept it when it's presented.

We've discussed looking at our triggers. Your Warrior knows these triggers and is already suiting up, preparing. It knows a battle with the voices will eventually arise.

YOUR NEXT STEP

Let's circle back to Don. He effectively and efficiently demonstrated all four traits of a Warrior. He was disciplined to go through the rules of engagement and not start shooting at people, even though he might have felt his life was on the line. It takes resilience to remain vigilant while on watch day after day and avoid complacency. He had trained endlessly to execute the series of moves from observation of a threat to leveling his weapon ("instinct from training"). He was prepared for potential threats by setting up a quick reaction force. When it did not come immediately, he remained levelheaded and went with his backup plan to seek reinforcements.

If you don't do something actively, you will be stuck in your status quo. Some people are happy there. But if you are looking for more in life, let's do something about it.

This mind shift of deciding that you don't want to be prey for the Cousins anymore, that you want to be happy, or that you want to experience life will take effort on your part. You may wonder, *Retrain my brain? Is that even possible? Sounds like a lot of work.* Or *Sounds like a lot of hokum.*

The first step in rewiring the brain and strengthening our inner Warriors is to recognize our accomplishments. The voices are trying to concentrate on all our weaknesses, insecurities, and doubts. But we are now going in the opposite direction. I want you to recognize all the good things you have already done.

A colleague introduced me to Phil several years ago because she thought I'd enjoy his podcast. Phil, also a navy veteran, was plagued by impostor syndrome and needed a way to counteract those feelings. His friend challenged him to start a gratitude book, a book in which he writes and describes what he is grateful for and his daily wins. I recently reconnected with him and checked to see how the gratitude book habit was going. He told me, "What started as a ten-day challenge has been with me for the last ten years!"

He told me that when he feels impostor syndrome sneaking up on him, he goes to his gratitude book and reads what he has written. Suddenly, those feelings of "I'm not sure about this" turn into "Maybe I've got this." And do you know why? Science!

> **The first step in rewiring the brain and strengthening our inner Warriors is to recognize our accomplishments.**

Remember our "Science of Stickies" section in chapter 1? As we read what we have written, our brain remembers those feelings of elation and the obstacles that we have already overcome. And we realize we can do this!

WARRIOR EXERCISE

Write down your most recent win.

____

____

____

Again with the writing? Yes. Write it down. As your brain is remembering this win, it is probably replaying the action. Where you were, whom you were with, what you were wearing, and more importantly, how you were feeling.

When you visualize what you have written, your brain activates the same neural pathways it did when you acted. This is the first step in retraining your brain. The simple act of writing your win down alters your brain-wave activity and biochemistry. Science is cool!

YOUR HOMEWORK

It's time to build your Warrior. In this chapter, we discussed discipline, resilience, training, and preparedness. Your homework for the next two weeks is to write down one win per day. At first, you may find it difficult to find a win every day. If you're finding this task difficult, try redefining what "win" means to you. I'm reminded of Admiral William H. McRaven's "Make Your Bed," his commencement speech to the University of Texas. The speech's theme was that anyone can change the world; all you need is the courage to do it. And by making your bed every morning, you have accomplished your first task. Even if you have a miserable day, you have come home to a made bed. You can count this one small, mundane task as a win.

You might not sign a big client or a lucrative publishing contract. But if you make the calls that might lead to a client or work on a writing project, those are wins. And then there are days when life is difficult, and you want to stay in bed. But you don't. That's a win too.

Use the table at the end of the chapter. You can also download a copy at thewarriorframework.com/tools. I filled in days 1 and 2 for a sample. Some days are going to be awesome, and you might have several to write down. Wonderful!

Developing our Warrior traits:

- *Discipline.* For two weeks, each day you will spend a small amount of time thinking about a win. This builds consistency, which is a building block of discipline.
- *Resilience.* Wins are typically defined by overcoming an obstacle. When you write down your win, reflect on your resilience to overcome that impediment. On days you feel like you didn't have any wins, expand your definition of "win."
- *Training.* Each day you are purposefully making your brain replay what happened and find a win. You'll probably find it's easier on some days than others. Keep at it, and note if it gets easier by the end of the second week.
- *Prepared.* Within the next two weeks, what challenges or triggers do you have coming up? If there is something looming in the next few days, write it down in the table. This is your first opportunity to challenge your Mean Little Voice

and Sneaky Little Bastard. We talk more about dealing directly with the Cousins in the next chapter, but now you have the occasion on your calendar.

At the end of the two weeks, you should have at least fourteen wins—fourteen victories over some adversity. Your brain has started to look for the wins through increased discipline and training. You are starting to realize you are more resilient than you thought. Relish all that you have accomplished. Don't back down or shy away from it. Don't start getting all humble on me. Own your successes.

DAY	WIN	OBSTACLE OVERCOME	UPCOMING OBSTACLE?
EXAMPLE DAY 1	Finally called X client	Fear of rejection	On day 3, I have a meeting with client Y that will be difficult.
EXAMPLE DAY 2	Worked out for 45 minutes	I always think I'm too busy, but I made time and it felt great!	
DAY 1			
DAY 2			
DAY 3			
DAY 4			
DAY 5			
DAY 6			
DAY 7			
DAY 8			
DAY 9			
DAY 10			
DAY 11			
DAY 12			
DAY 13			
DAY 14			

5

TRAIN AND EQUIP YOUR WARRIOR: READY, PART 2

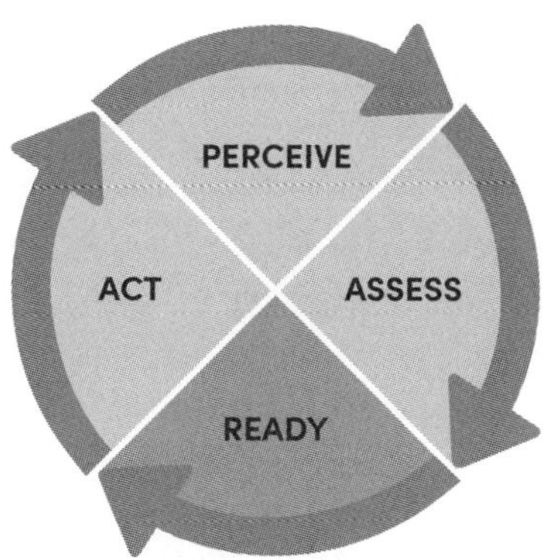

The whole convoy team's eyes were on me.

On speakerphone, the Afghan interpreter had just informed me that insurgents had infiltrated the general's unit. Several other coalition units around Afghanistan were on missions similar to ours. We were training their engineers, but the fledgling Afghan regime needed infantry, special forces, and a police force. From 2010 through our mid-deployment, there had been eighty-seven insider attacks by Afghan troops or ambushes by Taliban insurgents wearing their uniforms. These attacks had left 142 coalition troops dead and 165 wounded. Only three weeks earlier, US Army Major General Harold Greene was ambushed and killed at a training facility only a few miles from ours. So yeah, to find out there were insurgents in the unit we were about to drive out and train was an intense wake-up call.

The interpreter asked loudly enough for everyone to hear, "So are you coming out?"

The implications of my answer could mean life or death.

Time slowed waaaaaaaay down. When in a crisis, some people blank or freeze up. No thoughts. Nothing. That day, my mind went into a super-over-the-top, scrambled frenzy. There was too much noise in my head!

What's the right choice?
We are trained for this.
How did I get into this mess?
The interpreter said they caught all of them, so it's safe.
I suck as a leader.
I should say yes, but I'm scared.
You're too slow to answer.
I bet Commander So-and-So would know exactly what to say.

My thoughts flew as fast as leaves in a tornado, and I couldn't grab any of them. I knew some of those thoughts came from the Mean Little Voice, but it was all happening at once. I didn't have time to repeat my mom's mantra of "Are you going to let them beat you?"

Then I looked at my team. *Why are they all staring at me? Oh yeah, I'm their leader. Wait, that's it! My team!*

We had been through several serious situations and missions in the last three-and-a-half months. In each case, they had demonstrated keen decision-making capabilities. They were not only well trained, but they were also seasoned. I quickly started to run through all those other situations we had been in and how we had racked up successes. More importantly, I trusted them completely with my life. I also had my guardian angels, my personal security detachment, who performed their duties in an incredibly professional manner. The two of them went everywhere I went, always scanning for threats, their weapons at the ready. At times, they felt like overbearing dads.

Then something else clicked, like a domino falling into place. I had made challenging decisions before. This one might be the hardest, yet I knew I wasn't rash and would never purposely put my people in danger on a whim or for personal glory.

I don't know how many seconds it took for all this to happen. It felt like several minutes, but it wasn't too long because no one looked at me as if I had frozen. My second-in-command didn't nudge me or ask, "Ma'am, are you going to answer?"

I took a deep breath and calmly replied to the interpreter, "We'll be there."

I gathered the team in the parking lot and called in a few of our intelligence and defensive action experts. We revised how we would conduct security for the mission. We went out that day. And the next, and the next, until the end of deployment.

On an average day, it's easier to combat the voices. We have time and are not rushed to make decisions. We perceive and assess the voices for what they are and proceed to deal with them. As we discussed in chapter 4, your Warrior looks at the day and finds the potential battles. It prepares itself to face them using the techniques we are about to discuss. But when in a crisis, if your brain is not thoroughly trained, the voices find any crack and wind their way in. Like a dam, if we can't shore up those cracks quickly, they grow and can flood our minds.

In chapter 4, we met our Warriors. Now in the second part of step 3, "Ready," it's time to prepare them for battle. To ensure your Warrior is ready in everyday settings and in crises, you need three things: armor, strength, and weapons.

ARMORING YOUR WARRIOR

There are great warriors in many cultures: the Maori warriors, Scottish Highlands clans, Zulu of South Africa, Spartans of ancient Greece, and Vikings of Scandinavia.

I have always loved the samurais depicted in TV shows and movies. Great Japanese warriors, silent and lethal. And that armor? Dang! It always impressed me with its colorful, intricate layers. Each samurai's forty-five pounds of armor is composed of fifteen or more components, including the helmet, various guards, interlocking plates, and shoes. And every piece has a purpose.

Whatever Warrior best represents you, it needs armor. In your mind, that armor consists of recognizing and internalizing your achievements. We started this process in the previous chapters, and now we are going to use that knowledge to forge our armor.

Grab a new piece of paper and draw a vertical line right down the middle of your paper.

WARRIOR EXERCISE

On the left side of your paper, write down five of your accomplishments.

They can be whatever you like. Here are the two I always start with:

1. I was a US Navy captain, a rank only 3 percent of officers achieve.
2. I survived the master's and PhD engineering program at the University of California, Berkeley—and didn't become a hippie. (Maybe that counts as two accomplishments.)

Are we back to writing things down again? Yes. And I know it is easy, and you can do this in your head. But we need this list for our next exercise.

As you make your list (we'll get to the right side later), it can be anything, big or small. You made a great dinner last night. You killed it on a sales call yesterday. You won the fourth-grade spelling bee. This exercise should take you no more than about five minutes.

Figure 5.1 is a list of achievements I've collected from clients and audience members over the last couple of years. I hope this inspires you a bit. Notice that some are gargantuan achievements. Others are small and humble.

Made Commodore.
Finished marathon. Got a raise.
Awesome sales win. Went for a walk.
Exercised today. Signed up for training.
Hit sales quota. Decluttered my office. Started a company.
Paid off my loan. Learned to snowboard. Bought a house.
Raised good kids. Survived heart transplant. Meditated today.
4th Grade spelling bee. Got a masters.
Signed my first gig. Made sourdough starter.
Received promotion. Made a good dinner. Retired.
Took up a new hobby.
Became a pilot. Didn't kill my plants.
Finished my project.

FIGURE 5.1. WORD CLOUD OF ACHIEVEMENTS

What is the connection between armor and achievements? I'm glad you asked. I'm reminded of a childhood saying: "Sticks and stones may break my bones, but words will never hurt me." And my favorite: "I'm rubber; you're glue. Whatever you say, bounces off me and sticks on you."

We had these sayings because as children—well, let's face it: Kids can be cruel. These sayings were retorts and meant to not let the hurtful things others say affect us. But as adults, we say all kinds of mean and nasty things to ourselves. Your armor is the grown-up version of that mechanism. But you must *own* those achievements. Don't just skim over them and think just anyone could do them and that you aren't special. No, *you* did them. You overcame your battles for success. And when you do, the insults we tell ourselves will soon bounce off that armor.

STRENGTHENING YOUR WARRIOR

Warriors are strong. I'm not sure about you, but I haven't seen too many noodle-armed warriors. We need to be mentally strong and ready to combat the Cousins.

Warning: This may be the hardest lesson in the book. Don't back down. You are ready for this. I got you!

Take the piece of paper with your achievements. I want you to think about the how; how did you achieve what you have written?

> ### WARRIOR EXERCISE
> **On the right side of your paper, write down the "hows" to your top five accomplishments.**

You need just one how per accomplishment. But if you can think of more, write them down as well. It's fine if you have duplicates in the list. Take your time. Don't rush.

I recently did this exercise at a workshop for a corporate retreat. I asked one of the audience members, Ryan, "What was your most recent win?"

Ryan told me that he "killed it as the emcee for last night's dinner."

All his colleagues wholeheartedly agreed.

Then I asked him, "How were you able to do it?"

The swagger immediately gone, he looked at me sheepishly and shrugged. His eyes were downcast, the embodiment of humility. So I asked him some easy questions. "Do you have a good sense of humor? Are you quick-witted? Do you know the people

> **If you're like most people, you'll find it easier to remember negative thoughts or reactions about yourself than positive ones.**

around you well?"

He answered yes, with all his colleagues' heads bobbing in agreement.

"There you have it. You are humorous, clever, and perceptive."

His eyebrows lifted slightly, and you could see the realization settle in.

In this quick example, he had three hows for one achievement. If you are having difficulty producing one example, pretend you are describing someone who might have achieved that same accolade. It is often easier to see traits in others than ourselves. That shouldn't be a surprise. Think about it. If you're like most people, you'll find it easier to remember negative thoughts or reactions about yourself than positive ones. For example, you write a short story and ten people comment about it. Nine of the comments are positive. One is not. Because of the brain's innate negative bias, you will remember the negative more than the positive comment. Could you possibly learn something from that negative comment to make the story better? Sure. But I want you to start forcing yourself to give equal time and thought to the positive reviews.

When I think about the example of my top two achievements that I provided in the earlier section, I come up with this list of hows:

1. Resilience, dedication, loyalty, empathy, drive, humility, and willingness to sacrifice
2. Able to ask for help, grit, persistence, originality, and patience

Your hows are your inherent strengths. Just like your

achievements, I want you to *own* them as well.

Remember Anna and her marathon? She dreaded that race and what she feared she might become if she finished. She told me that she had never internalized how resilient and mentally strong she was just to get through the training phase, let alone the race. Anna, always on the hunt for a new goal and having learned how to push through the fear of success, has gone on to sign up for more wild events. She recently completed a two-mile open-water-swim race in Lake Superior. She experienced the same dread about the new identity she'd have if she finished, but each day, she got up and headed to the pool to practice. Eventually, when training required long swims in actual open water with a wet suit (which she had always thought only elite swimmers wore), she made herself swim with a group of triathletes who would swim in the open water of the lakes in Minnesota.

She had the same fears, but this time, she took stock of what she had already accomplished (her armor) and internalized her tenacity and belief in self. She knew she had done hard things before and could do them again (her strength). On race day, as she exited the water, the infectious smile that she beamed to the camera tells me she is ready for more.

We can be so hard on ourselves. The voices in our heads tell us we are not good enough, smart enough, or ready. But I want you to look at your list of hows. Really look at it. When we write things down, it becomes more real. Are you willing to accept these things about yourself? Are you smarter than you give yourself credit for? Are you stronger mentally and physically? Are you a pretty darn good leader? Are you great at creating and communicating ideas to your team?

This is not about being braggadocious or thinking too highly of yourself. You may even describe yourself as humble, so this exercise may be difficult. But don't take your humbleness to the point that you convince yourself that you are inadequate, void of gifts, or unable to recognize and voice the goodness within you. This exercise is about accepting your inherent strengths.

EVERY WARRIOR NEEDS A WEAPON

Some warriors need swords, others have shillelaghs, and a small cadre uses their hands as weapons (I'm looking at you, Bruce Lee).

When I showed up for Officer Candidate School (OCS) in Pensacola, Florida (boot camp for officers), it was a brisk January morning. On day two, I was greeted by Gunnery Sergeant Woollett, US Marine Corps. By the way, that's one word, all fourteen syllables: GunnerySergeantWoollettUnitedStatesMarineCorps. Not Gunny, not Gunnery Sergeant. No, it was all one word.

Why didn't we meet on day one? He would have scared the bejesus out of all of us, and we would have left. I know he wore a typical drill instructor's "Smokey Bear" hat, but I don't think I could describe more of him. I was either always on my face doing push-ups or maintaining a "thousand-yard stare." Even when he was in my face yelling at me, he would be just off to my left, in my periphery, because my eyes had to look straight ahead.

For weeks we trained, learning how to lead and how to march in a formation, learning what it was to be a US naval officer. There was a lot of running, lots of other calisthenics, and lots of what felt like torture from GunnerySergeantWoollettUnitedStatesMarineCorps.

When we neared the end of OCS, our next challenge came in the form of rifle drills. But these weren't the modern M16 or the small, lightweight M4 rifles we use in the military today. No, these were old-school M1 Garand World War II rifles with their barrels filled with concrete. Our modern M16 rifles weigh 6.4 pounds unloaded. The concrete-filled M1s weigh more than 11.3

pounds. They were heavy! I know this because as punishment one day for something someone did in our class, we had to do a wall squat (back against the wall, thighs parallel to the floor, shins parallel to the wall). But we got the added torture of holding our (insert your expletive of choice) rifles straight out with our arms parallel to the floor until GunnerySergeantWoollettUnitedStates-MarineCorps got tired.

During those last few weeks of OCS, we had special formation training with the rifles. We were instructed to carry our heavy weapons resting on our right shoulders at a forty-five-degree angle to the ground, right biceps tucked in tight, elbows at a ninety-degree angle, and right forearms very precisely parallel to the ground. Then it got really cool. We started doing drills: left shoulder arms, right shoulder arms, present arms, and order arms. By the end of the second week, GunnerySergeantWoollettUnited-StatesMarineCorps had us twirling our rifles. As a unit, we would never qualify as a silent drill team, but we also weren't horrible.

Of all the things I learned at OCS, this seemed the most frivolous. The running and calisthenics I understood made me faster and stronger. The classes we took were instrumental in preparing us to go out to the fleet. But marching around with heavy weapons and doing drills, how could that be relevant to anything I might encounter in the real navy? The weapons were outdated and useless. I also knew that the naval unit I was going to did not have a drill team.

I mean, yes, it did look pretty cool when we performed at our graduation ceremony. Parents and loved ones "oohed" and "ahhed" as we marched and twirled. But there was more to it than to show off. This was the military, and firearms needed to become extensions of ourselves. Despite growing up in Texas, my household did not own a gun. That stupid M1 Garand was the first weapon I ever touched. They were purposely heavy, which also made us stronger. These drills taught us precision, and it took an incredible attention to detail to get each movement correct. We learned to work with our guns as a unit. I also learned to take exceptionally diligent care of my weapon, lest I face the wrath of GunnerySergeantWoollettUnitedStatesMarineCorps.

So what is your Warrior's weapon of choice? It starts with that sticky note on your desk. In the previous chapter, we considered if the purpose behind the goal was enough to keep us motivated to pursue the changes we want in our lives. Without a strong why, it's hard to keep moving in the right direction when obstacles and setbacks occur. Your why is your greatest weapon.

I hope you have had time to think about your why.

WARRIOR EXERCISE

On your sticky note, under your goal or dream, write down your why. You can also write it here.

____

____

____

Your why can come from several reasons. Michelle, the pilot, was exhausted from the stress and facade she had created. Her why was based on improving her mental health and finding a sustainable way to complete her career.

Glenn, the dentist, had suppressed his trauma and knew his goal was to find a place of peace and healing within himself. He did this because he wants to grow and be a good dad and husband.

Anna had a goal of completing a marathon. Her initial why was to meet new friends. But there was also a deeper need to see if she could accomplish it. You have also met Paul, Greg, and Tammy. Each had their own goals and strong whys to pursue them.

If you are having difficulty vetting your why, ask yourself these questions:

In what way will your life be different if you achieve your goal?

- Will you be more financially secure?
- Will you have more flexibility?
- Will you finally be able to be yourself?
- Will you be happy?

Just like learning how to care for that M1 Garand, you need to learn how to be proficient with your why. When the voices come to attack, be able to draw up the why in your mind. Your why should be stronger than the vitriol that the malicious voices tell you. For instance, when the Cousins say that you are not ready/able/good enough to take that first step in pursuit of your dream, your why should remind you of the life that is waiting for you on the other side.

PULLING IT ALL TOGETHER

After years of believing that I had been a good-enough leader and could accomplish any mission, my self-image was broken by my tour in Afghanistan. I discussed my experiences earlier in the book, but to summarize, two of my bosses regularly told me that I sucked, my leadership style was insufficient, and I was worthless. That type of psychological warfare can get to you.

I had learned how to Perceive and Assess from the Warrior Framework, so I knew the voices I had were not instinct or intuition. But I needed more than a way to shield myself from them. I needed a way to *overcome* them. Whenever I started to feel the voices start their rants, I would go to the printer, grab a clean sheet of paper, and start writing down my accolades. I would list all of them that I could think of, including placing second in the third-grade science fair.

Over time, the list of accomplishments started to come to mind more easily. I had done these things. They were real, not made up like the voices and scenarios that played out in my head. I wasn't a complete failure. But I still felt there was more that I could do.

Then I remembered that during the ceremony where I handed off the battalion to my successor, I received several heartfelt notes, cards, and gifts from my troops and colleagues. For months, I had kept them in the closet. I couldn't bear to look at them and have the memories start to well up. I made myself pull them out and go through them. I would sit in my office reading them over and over. Many times, I would cry. OK, most times I would cry.

The notes from my troops became my anchor, grounding me further. My troops had cared enough to take the time to write how I affected their lives for the good. This is how people I cared about really thought of me. Their words weren't made up.

I decided I needed a new column on my hastily scribbled list of accolades. I wrote down a strength, a how, that my people saw in me. Just one. Something that others believed was true. The next day, I added a few more, and a pattern started to emerge.

I needed a way to *overcome* them.

I kept my list of accolades and strengths going, forcing myself to really see and internalize the words on the page. Every time the voices spoke up, I'd grab a piece of paper and start the exercise again. It got quicker, it expanded, and I created new patterns. That's when the last piece, which should have been obvious, clicked. I needed a why. So across the top of my scribbled accomplishments and hows, I'd write my why. Learn from my mistake. Always start with your why. Simon Sinek was right; always start with why.

I began doing this every week, whether the voices showed up or not. For example, when I knew I had something daunting coming up, like a contentious meeting, I'd sit down and practice. I thought about what I might feel and what my Mean Little Voice would say to me. I'd start with why I needed this meeting to go a certain way and then list all the work I had done for the project and how it had come together.

I later realized I was doing this exercise as a proactive step for any upcoming obstacle I might face, large or small. Hence step 3 of the Warrior Framework was born. Consequently, as I practiced this over and over, the Cousins became quieter and "visited" less frequently. I don't think it's just a coincidence.

MOBILIZE YOUR BATTLE BUDDY

Earlier in the book, I asked you to find a Battle Buddy. This is someone who knows you well. And here is the best part: A Battle Buddy can't hear your Mean Little Voice and Sneaky Little Bastard. I'm sure they have their own, but they can't hear yours and what they have to say.

The notes that I received from my troops spoke the truth, something far more tangible than the lies my Cousins were telling me. If you find yourself in a place where you can't distinguish the truth from the lies you tell yourself, please talk to your Battle Buddy or a mentor.

You don't have to make it all emotional and give your chosen Battle Buddy your life story. Just ask, "What do you think about this?" If the person is a true Battle Buddy, you'll get the truth.

> **A Battle Buddy can't hear your Mean Little Voice and Sneaky Little Bastard.**

My best friend in the military is Doug. We were both in the same unit when deployed to Iraq, and we have been each other's Battle Buddy to this day. Doug knew there was something wrong with me when I returned from my deployment to Afghanistan, but he gave me space to start working it out. When I finally told him all that went wrong there, he just listened. Yes, there was crying involved, again. But he listened. And when I was done, he just said, "Well, they're wrong."

Wait, that's it? He had known me for years, had served with me, knew the people who served under me, and just said, "They're wrong."

Find a Battle Buddy who will help you to find the truth when you feel like you are faltering.

TRAINING AND DISCIPLINE

As you look to embark on your goals, you may also have to deal with self-doubt and a lack of confidence. It might feel like life has been piling on, and you just want to move in a different direction. Or you may be in a good place and just need that extra "bump" for motivation.

You now have the tools to equip, strengthen, and arm your Warrior, and it's time to put them into action. Sounds easy, but how do you do it? Training and discipline.

We talked about these two principles in chapter 4, and we are now putting them to work. Your why may evolve over time, getting stronger, or you may find additional motives or deeper meaning. Think of this process as sharpening your weapon.

Our armor and strength need constant improvement if we are going to transform from a reactive to a proactive mindset. If you have ever played an instrument, you learned how to be more proficient by repeatedly playing the scales. In high school, I wanted to join the marching band. Unfortunately, my previous experience playing the piano and violin would do no good. I couldn't bring myself to play the xylophone, and there were no violinists out marching around under the Friday night lights on the football field. So I picked the clarinet. The clarinet is a beautiful instrument used equally in orchestras and jazz music. It has a full, rich sound when played by an expert. In the hands of a fourteen-year-old, it sounds like you are stepping on a duck. My poor family had to listen to me practice the scales repeatedly. Up and down, up and down the scales as my fingers learned to execute precise combinations to cover tone holes and use press keys and bridge keys while trying to force just the right amount of air through the reed and mouthpiece. Each pass up and down would build muscle memory. After a few months of scales, the band director finally gave us sheet music.

Like learning the clarinet, we are building muscle memory by recalling our achievements and strengths. With each pass of filling out the sheet with our why and then accomplishments and pairing them with our strengths, we are building the neural pathways to retrieve them easier and faster. Essentially, you are rewiring and training your brain to think in a positive direction. You will need this for your homework.

You are rewiring and training your brain to think in a positive direction.

YOUR HOMEWORK

I have provided a worksheet for you to write in your whys, accomplishments, and hows at the end of this chapter. You can also create your own or download one here: thewarriorframework.com/tools.

Consider five sets of accomplishments and strengths and then take a moment to fill this out twice a week for four weeks.

What? Four weeks?

Yes, filling it out once, as you may have done within this chapter, is not enough to create a new neural pathway. In high school or college, did you ever cram for a test the night before? You probably retained the information through the test, but most likely, you forgot it within a day or two. However, if you studied a bit every day, you probably retained the information longer. Scientifically, this is called spaced repetition learning. It's the same reason repeating something twenty times over one day is less effective than repeating something ten times in a week. Writing things down also creates a self-commitment.

There are more than one hundred thousand miles of nerve fibers that connect the various parts of the brain. These fibers govern what we think, feel, and perceive. Each time we have a thought, it travels the same path along our network of nerve fibers. Repeating a thought reinforces this pathway, making it easier for the brain to follow it.

If we want to replace an old thought with a new one, we must deliberately guide the new thought along a different route. This means that as a new thought is repeated, the neural components (axons, dendrites, and synapses) in your brain wire themselves together, strengthening the thought and memory. Although much research has been done on this, most scientists agree that it takes about thirty days of repetition to rewire the brain. Hence, I am asking you for four weeks.

I want you to be mentally strong. This is a goal you want very much, and I want to provide every tool for your use. This should only take about five to ten minutes of your day. Is your goal worth this small amount of time if it has the potential of a higher probability of success? Prominent neuroscientist Dr. Michael Merzenich states, "The harder you try, the more you're motivated, the more alert you are, and the better the potential outcome, the bigger the brain change. If you're intensely focused on the task and trying to master something for an important reason, the change experienced will be greater."

Most scientists agree that it takes about thirty days of repetition to rewire the brain.

But before you get started, you already have an initial advantage. I'm sure you have a few mighty accomplishments in mind. Well, in chapter 4 I had you write down one win per day, so you have more accomplishments to draw from. And I had you write down what obstacle you overcame. Think about how you overcame it, and voilà—there's your how/strength answer.

You will find as the weeks go by that there are new accomplishments you want to highlight and more strengths you have not explored yet. When you are ready, push for more than just five. Write as many as you can. Make it a game. Reward yourself afterward by treating yourself to something you enjoy.

This is your training, and it takes discipline to do this every week. You can do this. I have faith in you.

WARRIOR DEBRIEF

1. Your Warrior's armor is composed of recognizing and internalizing your accomplishments.
2. Your Warrior's strength is derived from your inherent strengths, strengths that you have repeatedly shown through your own accomplishments.
3. Your Warrior's weapon is your why, the strong purpose that drives you toward your goal.

WHY (WEAPONS) ____________________

ACCOMPLISHMENTS (ARMOR)	HOW (STRENGTH)

6

ACT LIKE A WARRIOR

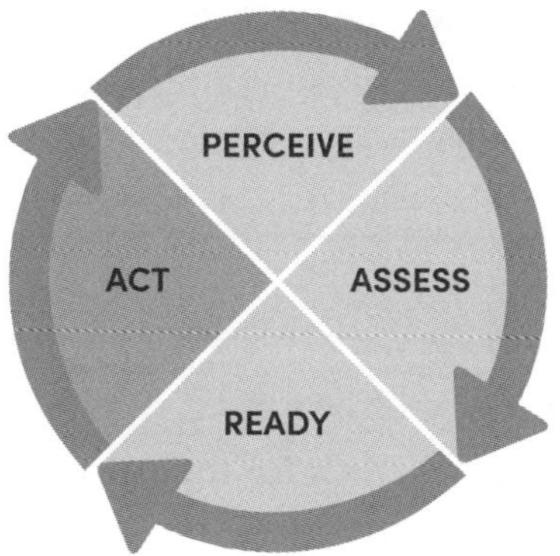

Eric always dreamed of being a writer.

At an early age, he had a habit of creating stories and imaginary conversations. He was ecstatic to be accepted to Eton, an English secondary school well known for its rigorous academic standards and notable alumni. It was here that he was exposed to a wide range of ideas and began to develop his own writing style. He wrote for the school newspaper, which helped hone his skills. Aldous Huxley, the author of *Brave New World*, was one of his teachers. Aldous spent time tutoring young Eric and had a significant impact on his literary development. Eric's early years at Eton were crucial in forming his early political views and his interest in social justice, themes that would become central to his work.

After graduation, Eric decided not to go to college or follow his dream. He took a different path and joined the Indian Imperial Police in Burma. During his five years there, he was exposed to the harsh realities of British colonial rule and the deep-seated racial prejudices that permeated the society. He resigned because of a growing disillusionment with British imperialism.

Returning to England, Eric chose to live in poverty to better understand the lives of the poor and marginalized. He worked as a dishwasher in Paris and wandered the streets of London. During this time, he was constantly poor. He returned to his roots and often relied on small writing jobs to make ends meet. He set small goals and started writing a series of essays and articles. Then he authored a book based on his own experiences with poverty and homelessness.

A few years later, he went to Spain as a journalist during the Spanish Civil War. Yet when he arrived, he immediately decided to enlist in the Republican militia for the Workers' Party of Marxist Unification. He spent time fighting on the front lines in Aragon and Catalonia. During April of that year, tensions began to rise between factions that made up the Republicans' alliance, each vying for power and their own idea of how the country should be ruled. In May, the hostilities boiled over into a series of street fights between rival factions. Though Eric was on leave, he flung himself into the fray, only for a sniper's bullet to rip through his throat.

Because of his wounds, Eric returned to England. It didn't take him long to figure out what his next move would be. He reconnected to what his life's goal had been all along, not just to become a full-time professional writer but also a writer who could change lives and the world around him. His why was to shed light on social injustices and political issues to make a difference in the world. That's a strong why! Sometimes a goal can linger until you are truly ready. His journey to find and define his why took time to develop. He'd had an incredible life filled with adventures and experiences he could use in his work. And he did all these things with tenacity and resolve. "Every line of serious work that I have written since 1936 has been written, directly or indirectly, *against* totalitarianism and *for* democratic socialism."

He again started small, writing memoirs and essays on politics and socialism. In 1945 and 1949, he wrote two of the most influential books of the twentieth century, *Animal Farm* and *1984*, respectively. His clear, direct style of writing and ability to convey complex political issues based on his life experiences have inspired countless writers, political movements, human rights activities, TV shows, and movies.

Eric's pen name was George Orwell.

Eric/George had been a semisuccessful writer earlier in his career. But it wasn't until he put all the tools together—his goal, his why, his accomplishments, and his how—that movement began on his career. What allowed him to become the seminal author of the 1900s was his ability to put these tools together and act.

WHY WE DON'T ACT

You've made it to the last step of the Warrior Framework. Hurrah! The mental aspect of dealing with the voices should be getting easier with each pass through your accomplishments/strengths worksheets.

Depending on your personality, this step, Act, may elicit nervous excitement or terrifying dread. But you have come all this way, and this is what we have been building up toward. Don't stop now.

There are many reasons why we might not take that first step toward our goal. The first might be fear. If this is true, I urge you to return to chapter 2, where we discussed the fear of failure and the fear of success. You are about to do something for yourself, something that you have always wanted to do. It's only natural that the Cousins may start to rear their ugly little heads again.

We might also make up excuses like, "I just don't have time." We have these incredible goals, but we get so wound up in our daily lives, work, deadlines, phone calls, conference calls, and other obligations that we forget to give ourselves a chance to just stop and think.

I need to get the kids to soccer practice.
I have a major deadline at 5:00 p.m.
We are out of milk, and I need to go to the grocery store, or I won't be able to cook dinner.

Sound familiar? I can't tell you how many times I get caught up with my ongoing commitments and forget to sit down and strategize. If you are currently caught up in the whirlwind of your life and feel that you are too busy to begin to act, ask yourself if this is somehow the work of the Sneaky Little Bastard. Is that voice creating reasons why you should not start? If so, work through the Assess and Ready exercises.

The third might be feeling overwhelmed. It may seem as though you are standing on one cliff, and across the chasm, you see your goal on the other side. But there is no bridge to get there. Depending on the size of your objective, the amount of time it will take, or the number of steps to get there, the enormity of it all may seem too great. Some of your goals may take years to accomplish. Other goals may require several intricate sequential or concurrent steps.

If you take a step in the wrong direction, it's all right. At least you are moving.

Authoring this book is a fitting example. Besides getting in my word count every day, there are so many concurrent activities: starting to work on the proposal, conducting interviews for stories, editing, building my email list, setting up podcast spots, thinking about what the workbook will look like, getting feedback from people who read prepublication copies of the manuscript, and strategizing LinkedIn posts. I know I have forgotten a few items. The entire process, from the ideation of the book until it is out in the world, is estimated to take about twenty months. It feels like, "Oh my gosh, that is forever." But then I look at the milestones and all that needs to be done, and it's a tight schedule. There are days when it would be so easy to be overwhelmed by all the various aspects.

The fourth reason you may not act might be uncertainty. It may be unclear what you should do first. You are excited and ready, but you look around and can't figure out which direction to go. Left? Right? Forward? Hopefully, it's not backward. You worry that if you go in the wrong direction to start with, it will be a waste of time or counterproductive. So instead of moving, you just stay put. We call this "paralysis by analysis." Look, you aren't surrounded by land mines. If you take a step in the wrong direction, it's all right. At least you are moving.

Whatever your reason for not acting, don't worry. I've got you. In the words of Dr. Martin Luther King Jr., "You don't have to see the whole staircase; you just have to take the first step."

George Orwell did not start out writing *Animal Farm* when he returned to England. In fact, he wrote two other books, several essays, and other articles. But he persisted and continued to write.

NO LEAPING INVOLVED

All right, I'll just come out and say it: I don't believe in leaps of faith. They're big, they're scary, and most of the time, they don't work. One major factor is the lack of preparation. Without proper planning and realistic expectations, unforeseen obstacles can arise, leading to failure. For example, let's say you abandoned your current life, forsaking everything, and moved to Los Angeles to become a big-time actor or actress. Besides the rare few who make it, there are more disappointments than success stories. That's the opposite of what we want.

Additionally, leaps of faith will call the Mean Little Voice and the Sneaky Little Bastard faster than kids to a candy store. Self-doubt and the fear of failure can paralyze and prevent you from fully committing to the leap. You sense the enormity of the leap you are about to take and realize you aren't a long jumper. As for me, I have the vertical leap of a sloth. I couldn't leap if I wanted to.

These often-spontaneous decisions rarely consider economic conditions or market trends. For example, the short-form video streaming service Quibi launched with great fanfare and substantial investment. However, it failed to account for the competitive streaming market and changing consumer habits, especially during the COVID-19 pandemic. The service shut down just six months after its launch.

Leaps of faith often underestimate the time, money, skills, or resources required to be successful. There are several reality TV shows in which people spontaneously buy homes with the plan to flip them quickly and amass a great financial windfall. Without the proper plans, budget, timetables, or general expertise, they wind up in financial hardship instead.

You are better than this. Your goal is worth it. And here are the tools to help you succeed.

ACT STARTS WITH A PLAN

In 2016, as I dreamed of becoming an entrepreneur, I realized that I didn't know where to start. From my cushy office in San Francisco, I knew there were several items that I needed to get started, including a good computer, an accountant, a website, a business license, an IT person, and start-up funds. From where I was to where I wanted to go seemed like an immense mountain to climb.

When I thought about my personal Mount Everest, I started to get anxious. When this happens, I get a sharp pain right between my shoulder blades that no amount of Motrin can help. It feels like someone stuck a knife in there, twisted it, and forgot to take it out. I'd lie awake at night, contemplating all the steps I had to take and playing out different scenarios in my head. The paralysis by analysis began to show up. Which direction first? Website, business license, new logo? And because I am pigheaded and like to figure out everything on my own, I didn't think to ask for help. So I was sinking deeper and deeper into the quicksand of my decision-making process. If I didn't act soon, I'd lose my nerve and never strike out on my own.

I knew I was starting to falter, so I swallowed my silly pride and turned to a mentor, Norm Abrahamson. He has worked with several of my independent contractor colleagues and had been one himself. I was having a challenging time working up the courage to talk to him on the subject. Norm is at the top of our profession, and I worried about what he would think of me; the Mean Little Voice had a few things to say about that. So I procrastinated in setting up a call, courtesy of the Sneaky Little Bastard.

I had been using the Warrior Framework over the last couple of months to ease the voices in my head following Afghanistan. When I heard the Mean Little Voice again, but this time for something completely unrelated, I wondered if that process could work in other areas of my life. As an experiment, I thought about calling Norm and making an appointment. Then I just listened.

Dadgummit! OK, that's not actually what I said, but I know my mom is reading this. It was the Cousins that were stopping me from my goal! They had found a new weakness and zeroed in on it. I had to go back to the basics of my accomplishments, how, and why. Sucking in a deep breath, I grabbed a fat red permanent marker and took my first step toward entrepreneurship. I circled a date on the calendar when I knew Norm and I would meet next. That would be the day—the day I would take my second step!

The fated red-circled day arrived. The anxiety knife was firmly rooted in my back, and it had brought along a few friends. Norm and I talked through all the normal engineering project technicalities.

Then I just blurted out, "I want to be an entrepreneur."

So much for my elegant, rehearsed speech that I had been practicing for a week. Norm was a bit taken aback but just nodded. He spent the next thirty minutes giving sound advice, recommending which action steps to take next, and most importantly, providing encouragement.

Planning is probably the most obvious but often overlooked piece of the Act step. I have found that there are three types of planners in the world: forward, backward, and no planners. This third group is called the "pantsers" because of their love of flying by the seat of their pants. Most pantsers never achieve their goals, or if they do, success takes longer because they wander around, trying this and that, and have no established deadlines or milestones. If you fall into this group, we'll work on a plan to convert you to one of the other categories and set you up for greater success.

Forward planners see their goal in the distance but

concentrate on looking at where they currently are and what their first step might be. They design their path sequentially, step after step, building momentum until the goal is reached. In contrast, backward planners typically break their goal into activities and then smaller components until they have a manageable task as the first step. It doesn't matter whether you are more comfortable planning forward or backward. You may need to make a pass both ways.

The best-made plans have seven elements. It's time to act like a WARRIOR:

Write
Action Plan
Resources
Review with Your Battle Buddy
Inspire Yourself
Overcome Obstacles
Resolve

WRITE

The first step is to write. As we discussed in earlier chapters, writing your goal, your why, and now your plan will solidify your commitment. You have already taken this step with the first two items; they are the sticky notes on your desk. Now we use this technique in the following steps.

ACTION PLAN

We need to develop a detailed action plan for achieving your goals.

Let's use my example for the first steps of entrepreneurship. As I summarized previously, there were several tasks that I had to do logistically and administratively. Some of these were of higher priority than others. For example, I didn't necessarily need to choose my preferred font and color palette on the first day. My first step was to make an appointment with Norm. After that appointment (step 2), he helped me to line up several follow-on action steps.

Make your first step so incredibly easy that it seems almost silly not to take it.

Here's how I break down a major goal. First, I write down all the major milestones that I know of on the way to reaching my goal. Then I look at the first one and break it into small, manageable tasks. I try to be as detailed as possible. Brainstorm this first milestone as thoroughly as possible. Chances are you will not yet know every task, or a new task might pop up when you are in the middle of the milestone. That's OK. But try to get to a place where you feel like you know at least 90 percent of everything needed to accomplish the milestone. Write these tasks down on a milestone tracker like I show in Table 6.1.

Now consider the other milestones. You don't need to break down the remaining milestones to the same level of detail as the first one. Your second, third, and each subsequent milestone will be less detailed and fuzzier than the previous one. Again, this is perfectly normal. Brainstorm all possible tasks within the milestones to the extent you can extrapolate into the future. Think of trying to find at least 75 percent of the tasks for the second milestone. Maybe the third will only be 50 percent.

Here's a tip: Make your first step so incredibly easy that it seems almost silly not to take it. If your ultimate goal is to learn how to skydive, make that first step to just go on your phone or computer and look up companies that teach skydiving. It's easy, takes no time at all, and has no consequences. Easy peasy, lemon squeezy.

Develop reasonable deadlines for each task. This is important! Again, start small. I know you are excited and ready to go, but try not to make your deadlines too aggressive. If they are, you have a higher probability of not meeting deadlines, getting behind, and eventually giving up. It's tough to come from behind and make up time toward a deadline.

This is not a failure; it's a learning experience to improve your ability to estimate time requirements.

You also have a higher chance of running out of motivation. Have you or someone you've known had a New Year's resolution to lose weight and signed up for a gym membership? How did it go? In a gym membership retention study by SHC, 50 percent of new members quit within six months, most after just ninety days. This is usually because they have unrealistic goals and timelines for losing weight. They go to the gym every day and are burned out in a few weeks.

Set a doable deadline. If you miss the mark, don't give up. And be on guard, as this could be a good time for the Mean Little Voice to sneak in and say *I told you so*. Instead, redefine what would be reasonable and work toward your new time frame. This is not a failure; it's a learning experience to improve your ability to estimate time requirements.

RESOURCES

Identify and gather the necessary resources (time, tools, support) to accomplish your goals. For me, making that appointment with Norm required courage. But other tasks, such as setting up a bank account for the business, required corporeal items.

As you go through this exercise of detailing your milestones, I want you to look for long lead-time items. The last thing you want to do is have a task in the last milestone that required you to do something six months prior. For instance, as I went through the first pass of my milestones, I needed several items for "Set up bank account." One of those was an Employer Identification Number (EIN), also known as a Federal Tax Identification Number, from the Internal Revenue Service (IRS). This activity would take at least eight weeks. To not delay future tasks, I needed to start that process early.

Also consider if you need to rely on other people, agencies (like the IRS), and processes that you have no control over. While these can play havoc with your timelines, do your best to estimate a reasonable length of time. Subsequent tasks may be affected, so provide lenient time frames for them as well.

Writing down the milestones, activities, and resources needed will help you stay organized. Trying to remember what step goes where and when to start it can quickly lead to overwhelm.

STEP DESCRIPTION	DUE DATE	RESOURCES?	DID I TELL MY BATTLE BUDDY (YES/NOT YET)?	ANTICIPATED REWARD	COMPLETE (YES/NOT YET)?
MAKE AN APPOINTMENT WITH NORM	November 1	Courage			
MEET WITH NORM	November 14	Open mind, paper, pen			
LOOK UP SMALL BUSINESS ADMINISTRATION	December 5	Spreadsheet to track what files I need			
SET UP BANK ACCOUNT	January 3	Name of business, EIN, start-up funds			

TABLE 6.1. INITIAL MILESTONE SETUP

I have provided a similar table for your use at the end of the chapter. It is also available as a digital download here: thewarrior-framework.com/tools.

Take a few minutes to write down the first couple tasks you need to do, and fill out the next two columns. If you are like me and need guidance, find a mentor or friend who can help you.

REVIEW WITH YOUR BATTLE BUDDY

In setting up my new business, my Battle Buddy was my husband. He was and is my greatest supporter. Each Friday, I'd give him an update on what I had accomplished and what I planned to do the next week. It was casual and typically done over a beer after work.

Like mentors, it's all right to have more than one Battle Buddy. For business, it's my husband. For military issues, it's my friend Doug. You may find that you need a few Battle Buddies for different areas of your life.

Your Battle Buddy is your superpower for achieving goals. In chapter 3 of Shawn Achor's book *Big Potential*, he describes a social behavior experiment he performed on a group of US Marine Corps soldiers at Camp Pendleton. He asked them to judge how steep a hill was. Seems straightforward. But when they described a hill while standing next to someone they considered to be a friend, the hill looked 10 to 20 percent less steep. When we have someone who supports us in our endeavors, even physical success such as climbing a real mountain seems easier and more achievable. Imagine the obstacles you will overcome with your Battle Buddy on your journey to your goal.

In chapter 1, I introduced you to the "Science of Stickies" and the work done by Dr. Gail Matthews of the Dominican University of California. In the first part of her study, she found that people who wrote down their goals were more likely to achieve them than those who simply thought about them. So we are already winning.

> **Your Battle Buddy is your superpower for achieving goals.**

In the second half of her research, and shown in Figure 6.1, she found that those who wrote down their goals and shared them with a friend—for example, a Battle Buddy—had a slightly greater advantage. But those who not only shared their goals but also provided weekly updates had a 15 percent higher success rate than those who kept their goals to themselves.

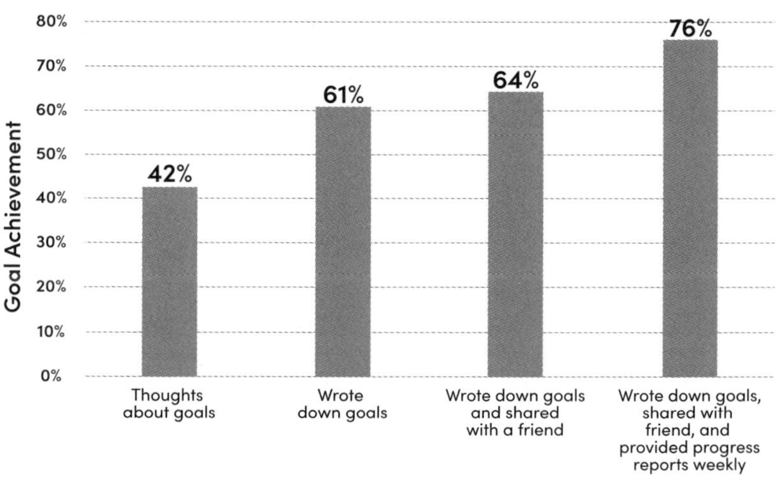

FIGURE 6.1. GOAL ACHIEVEMENT BY CATEGORY

Take a moment to update the next column of your milestone chart. Once you get started on your goal, regularly review your progress with your Battle Buddy. Depending on the time estimated to reach your goal, this may be weekly or monthly. Find a frequency that works best for you. Your touchpoints could be a phone call, text, or email. Or a casual discussion over a beer. You do you.

I recommend that you discuss three things:

- What you accomplished this week.
- What you plan to accomplish next week.
- Any issues or problems; your Battle Buddy can be a great sounding board for ideas.

STEP DESCRIPTION	DUE DATE	RESOURCES?	DID I TELL MY BATTLE BUDDY (YES/NOT YET)?	ANTICIPATED REWARD	COMPLETE (YES/NOT YET)?
MAKE AN APPOINTMENT WITH NORM	November 1	Courage	Yes		
MEET WITH NORM	November 14	Open mind, paper, pen	Not yet		
LOOK UP SMALL BUSINESS ADMINISTRATION	December 5	Spreadsheet to track what files I need	Yes		
SET UP BANK ACCOUNT	January 3	Name of business, EIN, start-up funds	Yes		

TABLE 6.2. MILESTONE CHART WITH BATTLE BUDDY INFORMATION FILLED OUT

INSPIRE YOURSELF

Stay inspired and motivated by visualizing your success and reminding yourself of your why, the reasons behind your goals. And while you're at it, celebrate your wins.

Research by Harvard Business School found that seemingly minor events at work have a major impact on people's emotions, perceptions, and motivations. Of these minor work events, the most impactful were “small wins.”

When I started my business, I didn’t just walk into my boss’s office one day, quit, and then hang my shingle the next day. My first step was working up the courage to talk to Norm about what it meant to be an entrepreneur. After making that decision, I went home and had a little celebration. For me, that was putting on my headphones and enjoying a leisurely walk around the neighborhood.

Based on the conversation I had with Norm, I worked on research with the Small Business Administration and started setting up the business bank account. I also predesigned how I would celebrate each step.

Step after step. Celebration after celebration.

You see, your brain is wired to respond to rewards. These small wins release dopamine, which is produced in the brain’s hypothalamus. This release boosts one’s attention, mood, and motivation. This, in turn, increases confidence and sense of accomplishment.

STEP DESCRIPTION	DUE DATE	RESOURCES?	DID I TELL MY BATTLE BUDDY (YES/NOT YET)?	ANTICIPATED REWARD	COMPLETE (YES/NOT YET)?
MAKE AN APPOINTMENT WITH NORM	November 1	Courage	Yes	Go for a walk	
MEET WITH NORM	November 14	Open mind, paper, pen	Not yet	Go out to dinner	
LOOK UP SMALL BUSINESS ADMINISTRATION	December 5	Spreadsheet to track what files I need	Yes	Have ice cream after dinner	
SET UP BANK ACCOUNT	January 3	Name of business, EIN, start-up funds	Yes	Have a glass of champagne	

TABLE 6.3. MILESTONE CHART WITH REWARDS FILLED OUT

OVERCOME OBSTACLES

There will be bumps in the road. We need to anticipate potential challenges and plan strategies to overcome them. This is where risk comes in.

In business, we throw the word "risk" around a lot, especially when talking about potential projects. I used to work on the seismic hazard for dams. More specifically, I would calculate what the impact of an earthquake would have on the dam's structural stability and functionality. We had a lot of fancy equations, and you needed some higher-end math to calculate the exact risk number. Some industries use a risk matrix, like the one shown in Figure 6.2, to assess the level of risk. But if you boil it down, risk is just the probability that something will go wrong and the consequences if it does.

Consequences

Likelihood	NEGLIGIBLE	MINIMAL	MEDIUM	MAJOR	CATASTROPHIC
ALMOST CERTAIN					
LIKELY					
POSSIBLE					
UNLIKELY					
RARE					

FIGURE 6.2. RISK MATRIX

In Figure 6.2, low, medium, and high risk are shown as light, medium, and dark gray, respectively. By the way, you can use this figure for your goal, or you may apply its principles to steps and activities along the way.

If you are still worried that the pursuit of your goal may be lined with failure, let's look beyond failure and instead consider risk. Here are a couple of quick examples:

- Let's say your goal is to learn how to play checkers. This is a rather simplistic game often played by children as young as four years old. The probability that you will fail to learn checkers is low; it's very easy. We would categorize this as a "rare" likelihood. The consequences of not learning to play are also pretty low; your world won't change much. Your consequences would be "negligible." Low probability, low consequence, hence low risk.
- But let's say your goal is to get rich. You sell your house and car, empty out your bank accounts, and play the lottery. The probability that you will

> fail to win the lottery is massive; the odds of succeeding are only 1 in 292,201,338.* Your likelihood of losing is "almost certain." The consequences if you do not win the lottery are "catastrophic" because you liquidated assets to buy lottery tickets and will have nothing left. High probability, high consequences, hence high risk.

I'm sure the Mean Little Voice has already helped you brainstorm all the obstacles and things that could go wrong. It is often called catastrophizing when we jump to the worst possible conclusion and treat it as being likely. But let's take a step back. How probable are those scenarios? What you may find is that although you have come up with a bunch of "catastrophic" endings, the likelihood that they will happen is "rare" or "unlikely."

If you fall into the low-risk category, go for it, and don't look back. If you know the risk will be medium or high going in, you can set up safeguards and safety nets. Let's take our lottery example. This is a high-risk activity, and you might lose everything. Your fallback plan might be to work it out with your parents to stay in their basement for a few years until you get back on your feet. Again, just because the risk is high doesn't mean you stop. Instead, you design backup plans and institute controls.

Figure 6.2 is a modified and simplified version of the operational risk management (ORM) system used by the military. We look at a mission, break down the components, and apply ORM to

---

* For all the math lovers out there, if you have five white balls numbered 1 to 69, the combination formula is C(69,5) = 69! / [5!(69-5)!], which equals 11,238,513. Then multiply this by the red Powerball with 26 options, and you get 292,201,338. Math rocks!

each. An example might be complex, like planning a convoy. Or it could also be as simple as needing to use a ladder or planning for inclement weather. If the activity is considered high or medium risk, we don't just throw our hands up and say, "Oh well. I guess we aren't doing that." No, the mission needs to be completed, just like your goal, and we look to lower the risk through three methods:

- *Engineering controls:* These focus on designing or modifying equipment, processes, or environments to reduce or eliminate hazards. For the convoy scenario, if you are worried about improvised explosive devices buried in the road that could cause damage or death, an engineering control might be to limit the speed of the convoy so that the electronic warfare equipment can more easily detect them. Maybe you have an easier scenario in that you need a very tall ladder to work on something at a great height. An engineer control would be to modify the equipment and set up scaffolding instead.
- *Administrative controls:* These are procedures and policies designed to reduce risk by managing how tasks are performed. An administrative control might be to change the policy for work schedules. When we were in Iraq in July, it was 118 degrees by 9:00 a.m., and I really didn't want to know how hot it got. Our initial work hour policy was from 7:00 a.m. to 7:00 p.m. Not wanting to cause undue harm to our troops by making them work through the hottest part of the day, we modified the policy and worked incredibly early in the morning,

or sometimes through the night when it was much cooler.

- *Personal protective equipment (PPE):* This control involves using specialized gear, such as hard hats and gloves, to protect personnel from hazards.

I'm not trying to make you into a military ORM professional. God knows you have other things to do with your life. I provide this information so that you understand how others look at the potential for failure and what to do about it.

Let's go back to our stickies. Say that your goal is to go back to school to get a master's degree. You have divided your goal into different components, such as researching schools for a good fit, filling out applications, passing the proper entrance exam (GRE, GMAT, LSAT, MCAT*), determining a budget, and so on. We can perform a risk analysis on each part. For example, we need to pass the GRE. Without studying, there is a good chance that you might fail, so we assign this as a "likely" probability. If you don't pass, you won't be accepted, which would be "catastrophic." This then qualifies as a high-risk activity. You can fill out each component toward your goal in Table 6.4, also provided at the end of the chapter and here: thewarriorframework.com/tools.

---

* Graduate Record Examination (GRE), Graduate Management Admission Test (GMAT), Law School or Medical College Admission Test (LSAT or MCAT).

COMPONENT	LIKELIHOOD	CONSEQUENCES	RISK LEVEL
PASS GRE	Likely	Catastrophic	High-Risk

TABLE 6.4. RISK TABLE 1—RISK LEVEL ANALYSIS

Applying our ORM, we have several engineering controls we could use:

- Choose a quiet, distraction-free area to study.
- Find apps and software for GRE preparation.
- Utilize a virtual study group or forum to collaborate with.

Our administrative controls could be:

- Designate time each day to study. This could be early in the morning before work, or after the kids go to bed. Find a time that is open and you will not be disrupted.
- Set an alarm on your phone as a reminder to study.
- Set milestones to complete certain subjects.

Our PPE control:

- Use noise-canceling headphones to minimize interruptions.
- Consider ergonomic accessories, such as chairs and keyboards, to make things more comfortable.
- Use your armor. When you start to forget everything you have done so far, remember your past achievements. You can do this!

Now fill out Table 6.5 with your own controls, also available at the end of this chapter and here: thewarriorframework.com/tools.

COMPONENT	ENGINEERING CONTROL	ADMINISTRATIVE CONTROL	PPE CONTROL
PASS GRE	Get the GRE App	Alarm set for 7 a.m.	Noise-Canceling Headphones

TABLE 6.5. RISK TABLE 2—RISK CONTROL ANALYSIS

RESOLVE

It's time. That first step on your plan may feel like the hardest. As Thomas Fuller, the eighteenth-century physician, included in his book of popular sayings, “All things are difficult before they are easy.” You probably feel like you are just standing still, melting into the quagmire of your status quo. Taking that first step requires courage, but it also means you must do something! It will take commitment to shift from stationary to mobile.

Courage is a choice.

There are two types of courage: physical and moral. Physical courage deals with the threat of death, physical pain, and hardship. Consider running into a burning building to rescue someone. Moral courage gives you the ability to face scandal, loss, shame, opposition, or discouragement. This is the courage that many of us need to make a change in our lives to follow our dreams or goals.

Whichever type of courage you are looking for, you need to find your spark, your why, to move forward. Having courage doesn’t mean you are never afraid. It means that even when you are scared, terrified, or even petrified, you summon your courage and continue anyway.

From courage comes confidence, which keeps you moving. As you work through your goal, make sure to change that last column from “not yet” to “yes.”

STEP DESCRIPTION	DUE DATE	RESOURCES?	DID I TELL MY BATTLE BUDDY (YES/NOT YET)?	ANTICIPATED REWARD	COMPLETE (YES/NOT YET)?
MAKE AN APPOINTMENT WITH NORM	November 1	Courage	Yes	Go for a walk	Yes
MEET WITH NORM	November 14	Open mind, paper, pen	Not yet	Go out to dinner	Not yet
LOOK UP SMALL BUSINESS ADMINISTRATION	December 5	Spreadsheet to track what files I need	Yes	Have ice cream after dinner	Not yet
SET UP BANK ACCOUNT	January 3	Name of business, EIN, start-up funds	Yes	Have a glass of champagne	Not yet

TABLE 6.6. MILESTONE CHART COMPLETED

You can cultivate the courage and determination necessary to face challenges head-on and persist through difficulties.

PLAN BUT MAINTAIN FLEXIBILITY

As Jamie and her family got off the plane in Costa Rica, fatigued after seven hours of travel, the squeals of delight and ensuing hugs from her awaiting siblings, aunts, uncles, cousins, and their kids made up for all the hassles and flight delays. After the kisses and the "Oh, it's so great to see you alls" were complete, an itinerary was thrust into her hands. For the next three days, each hour had been planned in meticulous detail. Sure, there were options. For example, at 3:30 p.m. on Saturday, she could zip-line through the trees or kayak through the mangroves. But otherwise, her aunt ran a tight ship.

Jamie had been working fifty and sixty hours a week

recently and had never been to Costa Rica. She looked forward to a few peaceful hours of lounging on the beach. Maybe she would finally get a chance to read her book or just simply take a nap. Unfortunately, there was no lounging time on the itinerary. But she knew this going into a family vacation. Her aunt was an insatiable planner, and there was no crossing the matriarch of the family.

Halfway through the second day, her husband, Mick, tired of the strict schedule and wanting to do something that he might enjoy, looked at his haggard wife. He walked over to the itinerary and ripped it down the middle. Jamie and their two kids stared open-mouthed at Mick as if he had just desecrated an ancient temple.

"Your family will forgive us," was all he said.

Having a plan is critical for achieving your goals. But don't make it so strict that you have no maneuverability. I've seen clients put together incredibly detailed plans. When they don't meet one of those milestones, they throw their hands up in the air and label themselves failures, followed by abandoning their goals.

Don't be Jamie's aunt and create such a rigid plan that you have no means to see the alternatives that might be possible. There may be better options and action steps than what you initially thought.

The US Marine Corps's motto is "Semper Fidelis"—Always Faithful. But the rest of the military has modified this saying into "Semper Gumby*"—Always Flexible.

---

* For those who may be unfamiliar, Gumby was a green-clay, stop-action, animated character first introduced in the early 1950s.

FIGURE 6.3 PATCH OF THE SEMPER GUMBY

In the military, we know everything will not go exactly to plan. You are told to attend a meeting at 1500 (or 3:00 p.m.), yet something comes up, and whoever called that meeting is thirty minutes late. Semper Gumby. You are told to take a unit to one location, but at the last minute, you must switch to a new one. Fine. You can either get upset about it, or you can go back to the drawing board and change your movement plan. Semper Gumby. We use this mentality to make decisions and adapt quickly to changing conditions.

Build flexibility into your plan by giving yourself extra time between milestones and action steps. In the construction world, this is called "float." It gives you leeway if one milestone runs long so that it doesn't impact future activities. This creates less stress and keeps you motivated.

Allow yourself to adjust as needed to stay on track. The paper of this book and the downloadable files are not made of stone. That would make things too heavy and cost prohibitive. So, too, is your path to your goal; you didn't write it in stone. It's *your* plan, so modify it to your heart's content.

You will need all these tools if things go sideways or even terribly wrong.

As you set off on your journey, remember that the second half of Dr. Martin Luther King Jr.'s quote is "with faith, you will reach your destination if you keep taking step after step."

WARRIOR DEBRIEF

1. There are many common reasons why people hesitate to act, including being fearful, making excuses, and feeling overwhelmed and uncertain.
2. Act has seven elements: writing down goals, creating action plans, identifying resources, reviewing progress with a Battle Buddy, staying inspired, overcoming obstacles, and maintaining resolve.
3. Move beyond thinking of failure and instead consider risk.
4. Build flexibility into your plan.

MILESTONE CHART

STEP DESCRIPTION	DUE DATE	RESOURCES?	DID I TELL MY BATTLE BUDDY (YES/NOT YET)?	ANTICIPATED REWARD	COMPLETE (YES/NOT YET)?

RISK TABLE—PART 1

COMPONENT	LIKELIHOOD	CONSEQUENCES	RISK LEVEL

RISK TABLE—PART 2

COMPONENT	ENGINEERING CONTROL	ADMINISTRATIVE CONTROL	PPE CONTROL

7

FAILURES, SETBACKS, AND NAYSAYERS

My first month as an entrepreneur, I was a little cocky. I was extremely proud that I had done it. I was my own boss! *Woo-hoo! This is awesome!* I had secured contracts with my former company, and I had a healthy number of people inquiring about my engineering services.

Four months went by—and those same contracts were ending. My calls of inquiry had not materialized into anything solid. Sure, people wanted to collaborate with me, but they didn't have a budget available for their current projects, and I would have to wait until they bid on new jobs.

Six months went by, and I sat on the floor of my little office and cried. The Mean Little Voice whispered over my shoulder, *I told you so. No one wants to work with you. You will be the ruin of this family.*

My cavalier attitude toward running a business was: (1) encounter a problem, and then (2) figure it out. I had failed to be proactive in bringing on clients and learning about marketing. I had no short-term, long-term, or strategic plans. As my drill instructor would say, I waded into entrepreneurship like John Wayne without a jockstrap. I had successfully figured out how to get the business up and running. I had not figured out how to keep it running.

We have all kinds of plans in the military: primary plans, branch plans, backup plans, strategic plans, tactical plans, plans, plans, plans. We know they are not flawless and often use the saying, "All plans are perfect until the first shot is fired."

Now that does not mean the military is horrible at planning; it's quite the opposite. In battle, there are always uncontrollable factors and variables. Because of this, the military has designed a robust methodology to prepare for each aspect of a campaign. The Marine Corps Planning Process (MCPP; pronounced McPee-Pee, which always elicits a few giggles) is the most popular among those in the navy and taught to every officer and senior enlisted.

The brilliance in the MCPP is how it's structured. There is a white cell and a red cell, military terms for a group of good guys and bad guys, respectively. The white cell develops the strategy, and then the red cell (or the presumed enemy) pokes holes in it. The proposed plan is "war gamed," each cell against the other, to figure out all possible outcomes. The results are used to create branch plans or backup plans. In the worst cases, you go back to the drawing board. This process allows troops to switch quickly and further confuse the enemy.

Why all this talk about plans? Unfortunately, the world is not made of rainbows and unicorns. There will be failures, setbacks, and naysayers along your journey, so you need to be prepared.

We do need a solid path forward with a few preplanned reroutes.

You may be wondering, *But wait. I just got through dealing with all the internal stuff, and now I have to deal with the external stuff as well?* It's OK. You are in good hands. What you need is a plan to deal with adversities.

In the words of Rear Admiral Josh Painter from the movie *The Hunt for Red October*, "Russians don't take a dump, son, without a plan." We are not going to go to those extents, but we do need a solid path forward with a few preplanned reroutes. Consider your road map as a "choose your own adventure." Something happens, and you need to pivot. An obstacle surfaces, and you execute a spin move.

IS YOUR GOAL WORTH IT?

Here's the thing. Almost everyone fails the first time they try something. For example, the first time you strapped on your skis or snowboard, did you go down a black diamond? Probably not, at least not on purpose. Even heading down the bunny slope might have been difficult that first day. If your goal is to learn how to ski, the prudent thing to do is to get an instructor. When you fall or when you fail, instructors are there to encourage you to get back up, learn from your mistakes, and keep trying.

My mom put me on skis when I was six years old in Ruidoso, New Mexico. She told me to stand there as she worked on her boots and bindings, not realizing I was on a bit of a slope. Like any six-year-old, I started fidgeting, picking up one ski and then the next, hopping up and down. Suddenly, I started to move backward. I looked over my right shoulder to see what was behind me and the direction I was going. I was headed for a ravine. Instant panic erupted as I picked up speed. I dropped my ski poles, and my little mitten-covered hands started flailing.

"Mom!" I yelled. "Mom!"

"Just fall over, Jennifer! Fall over!"

At six years old, the ground is luckily not that far away, and I face-planted to stop my progression toward what seemed like a fifty-foot-deep ravine. My six-year-old self still traumatized, my mom hauled me back over the edge. I don't remember much of the rest of the day except hanging onto the tow rope for dear life as I was dragged up the slope on my back because I fell over and was afraid to let go and be run over by whoever was behind me.

For the rest of my youth, I would ski a day or two every couple of years. Each time I clicked my boots in, I would try to remember where I had left off a few winters previous. The inconsistency never allowed me to progress much past feeling semiconfident on a blue (medium-skill) slope. In contrast, my husband grew up next to a ski resort, and his mother was a ski instructor. For him, black diamond runs (the hardest) are too easy. We now live near a ski resort, and with more consistency and instruction from him, I am making steady progress. Some days are successful. Some are neutral. And then there are the days characterized by what skiers like to call having a yard sale, when you crash so violently that skis, poles, hats, mittens, and sometimes boots are scattered all down the slope.

Nearly careening into a ravine that very first day was only my first failure at skiing. I have fallen a lot. But one of my goals is to ski to the best of my ability. I will never be as good as my husband; I don't have the years of experience or the time to dedicate to being that good. But I can improve from where I am now. You may fail and fall, but the question remains: Will you get back up and keep trying?

Will you get back up and keep trying?

You have many responsibilities in your life, not just to yourself, but to those around you. When you fail, it will be easy to just quit and stay with your status quo. Trust me, there are a thousand excuses that will spring to mind: *Oh well, I gave it a shot. I guess it's not meant to be. It was not the will of the universe.*

It is times like these that I want you to look deep into your soul and answer this one question: Is your goal worth it?

If the answer is yes: Do. Not. Quit. Maybe you didn't have a proper plan, or inexperience got in the way.

If you fail, don't quit. Let's take Thomas Edison for instance. He tried for years to create a light bulb. He was once interviewed by a reporter who asked, "Mr. Edison, you have now tried ten thousand ways to create a light bulb and failed every time. What does it feel like to fail ten thousand times?"

Mr. Edison calmly replied, "Sir, I have not failed ten thousand times. I have merely found ten thousand ways that don't work."

This is such a better commentary on our *perceived* failures. They are just avenues that might have been a dead end. Time to circle back and find a new route.

When we fail, it often feels like our disaster is plastered all over the billboards. We feel ashamed, as if everyone knows about it and is judging us. Realistically, it might not be that many people, and the harshest critics will be ourselves.

But what happens when you fail in front of the entire world? At the 2024 Paris Olympics, the US male gymnastic team finally felt like it had put together the dream combination of athletes. Having failed to medal since 2008, this was their year. Brody Malone was expected to be one of the highlights for the team.

However, in the qualification round, he struggled with his two best apparatuses. He fell off the high bar twice and once off the pommel horse. The US men's team finished fifth in the qualifiers.

Imagine practicing your whole life to become one of your nation's top athletes. Endless days breaking down each routine, practicing this twist or that flip until they were perfect. So perfect that you beat out other gymnasts looking to participate on the biggest stage in the world. You were a national and world champion. But instead, you delivered one of the worst performances of your career. And since you are part of a team, your performance affects the outcome of your four other teammates.

What do you do? Brody had the mindset to not let failure define him. He acknowledged his mistakes but looked to the future. In an interview, he said, "You'll not always be perfect. So I'm just going to go reset tomorrow in the gym, reset my foundation with some basics and then just be ready for team finals." A few days later, Brody had a resurgence with nearly flawless routines. His scores alone helped boost the Americans from fifth place to a spot on the podium once again, with bronze draped around their necks.

Don't be hard on yourself for failing or falling, sometimes literally, like Brody. In addition to not dwelling on his failures, he had some great Battle Buddies. After the qualifiers, the commentators swirled questions at him about his aptitude and wondered whether he would be cut from the team. Quite the opposite happened. His teammates and coaches rallied around him, encouraging him. He didn't give the voices a chance to start speaking up. He was armored with the knowledge of all the work that had brought him to this point. He was mentally strong and knew what he was capable of, and he wielded his laser-focused goal to be one of the top gymnasts in the world.

This is all part of the journey and a true test of creating a Warrior Mindset. Pick yourself up, dust yourself off, learn from your mistakes, and continue.

> **Pivoting is not failure. Quitting is.**

Remember your training from the earlier chapters. Don't let the voices get through your armor. You know your past great achievements. If you need to, write down your accolades again, match them up with the hows, and recall your strengths. You are going after a change in your life, and you also have a strong why behind it. Use your why to plan a new way, a new path. Try using a branch plan or your primary plan again, but this time with more information.

There is a difference between failures and setbacks. A setback isn't a complete failure, but it may require you to reassess your direction. You may not have failures, but you may have setbacks. For the lucky ones, as they pursue their desired changes, the route may be straightforward. But for the rest of us, it's going to feel like a hedge maze. You go down one alleyway and meet a dead end. You may need to go back to the beginning and take another route. Pivoting is not failure. Quitting is.

I've had many setbacks. Going back to my skiing adventures, near the end of one season, I partially tore my rotator cuff. It was dumb. I was tired, and it was near the end of the day. I knew I was pushing myself past the point where I could recover. I didn't see the little kicker jump,* and I launched into the air. I soared, I swore, I flailed, and I somehow landed like a sack of potatoes on my left shoulder.

---

* A short, very steep, almost vertical jump.

After taking two weeks off, the next time I went up the mountain, I knew I had a major setback. I was visibly shaking as I slowly went down one of the easiest runs to get my confidence back up. My head was screaming, *Too fast! Too fast!*

I made it to the bottom of the run, panting, and knew that I had a choice to make. I could hang out in the nice warm lodge and drink hot chocolate while waiting for my husband to finish his day, or I could get back on the chairlift and do it again. I chose the chairlift.

As with failures, you have the ultimate choice to make: Use your setback as an excuse to not try again, or pick yourself up and find another way.

My friend Alison knows no bounds. She has climbed the highest peaks on every continent and skied to the North Pole and the South Pole. It's called the Adventure Grand Slam. In 2002, she became the leader of the first women's expedition up Mount Everest. As she described, besides the months of preparation, you don't just arrive at the Everest Base Camp, strap on the crampons, and start climbing. You start in Lukla, Nepal, at an elevation of 2,860 meters (9,383 feet) and hike 130 kilometers (80 miles), through five way stations to the Everest Base Camp at 5,364 meters (17,600 feet). You stay there for several weeks to acclimate to the conditions. There are nearby peaks to scale as you continue with the adjustment process. But otherwise, you bide your time looking up at the peak that's beckoning you to climb.

When it's finally time, you gear up and head to Camp 1 at 6,065 meters (19,900 feet). Though maybe a bit worn out, in the distance, you see Camp 2. And guess what? That's not where you are going. You turn around and go back down to base camp. Yep, the opposite direction of where you want to go. It's not a one-way trip. A few days later, you climb back to Camp 1, but this time, you get to spend a couple of nights there. *Awesome!* Now, on to

Sometimes you need to turn around, reassess, pivot, and then strike out again.

Camp 2? Nope. You descend back to base camp again. Spend a few more days acclimating and then back up to Camp 1. Then finally, you strike out for Camp 2 at 6,400 meters (21,000 feet). *Yay!* You spend a few nights and then head down. Where? Not to Camp 1, but all the way back to the base camp again. Up and down, up and down. The initial acclimation phase of going from Everest Base Camp to Camp 3 at 7,300 meters (24,000 feet) can take four to six weeks! When you are finally ready to summit and reach the world's highest peak at 8,848 meters (29,029 feet), that's another four to seven days.

Your setbacks are just like these trips back down the mountain. At first, the trek to your goal begins easily, but it can quickly get more difficult, especially the closer you get to reaching your goal. Sometimes you need to turn around, reassess, pivot, and then strike out again. Each time you do, you get stronger, you know where the pitfalls and crevasses are, and you are ready to keep striking forward.

THE NAYSAYERS

Ah, the naysayers. When it comes to sneaky, they may be sneakier than the Sneaky Little Bastard. Who are these naysayers? Most of the time, they are the ones closest to us. They may be spouses, loved ones, or best friends.

You have great responsibilities toward them, and they look to you for stability and to stay with the status quo. Some naysayers will intentionally try to sabotage you, while others, seeming to have your best interest in mind, will hold you back.

My dear friend Jacqui has an infectious laugh and an overly

kind and generous demeanor. I don't think I have ever seen her when she was not wearing something pink. It fits her lively, bubbly personality. With such an effervescent attitude, you would never know that Jacqui was raised in a household of domestic abuse. Her earliest memories were of fear and uncertainty. Moving around often due to a lack of jobs for her father only increased the stress on her family, which worsened with her parents' drinking and violence. The youngest of four kids, Jacqui, at the age of seven, was in and out of foster care, typically separated from her brother and two sisters. She felt alone, desolate, and stuck.

That was, until Jacqui met a new friend, Susan, when she was twelve. Susan's parents were divorced, but Jacqui told me, "They just seemed . . . normal." Was this what it was like to have a family with no yelling or abuse? Susan and her mom, Diane, also did something that had never happened to Jacqui; they believed in her. For the first time, someone saw something in her that nobody else had. Jacqui knew deep down it was there but didn't know how to express it.

Diane enjoyed sharing books with Jacqui, who felt honored that Diane considered her capable of appreciating the same literature. They also discussed topics that Jacqui might be interested in, like cooking and traveling. Nobody from Jacqui's family had ever done this or even tried. That's when Jacqui's perspective started to change. She began to believe in herself, knowing she was capable of so much more. She wanted to explore not only different aspects of her life, but she also wanted to go out and explore the world.

At the age of eighteen, Jacqui dropped out of high school and moved out of her parents' house into an apartment with her friend. She received immense pushback from her family. She was accused of trying to change the status quo. "Jacqui, you're abandoning this family! How could you possibly want to go somewhere else?"

The naysayers make *your* choices about *themselves*.

She now realizes that when she left, it forced her family to look at their own situations, which made her parents and siblings feel uncomfortable. It was easier for them if things stayed as they had always been, or at least seemed to have been. They wouldn't have to look into the dark, uncomfortable parts of their lives.

Jacqui earned a general educational development (GED) certificate. She eventually became a flight attendant and traveled the world, seeking adventures and seeing all the sights she dreamed of as a young girl. She helped grow her and her husband's extremely popular multimillion-dollar business. Her family still gives her grief from time to time, and they have never fully accepted the world she created for herself.

For Jacqui, the naysayers were intentionally cruel. Spreading their doubts in her abilities showed that they didn't want her to succeed because it would be a reflection on their own lives. She told me, "If you are in the situation where the naysayers are holding you back for their own selfish reasons, listen to your gut feeling. It is never wrong."

The naysayers make *your* choices about *themselves*, not about you. Remember that times may be difficult, or it may be hard to accomplish that goal or make that change, but you are doing it because it is the right thing for you. Jacqui successfully broke the cycle of violence that her family created. Her two sisters have noticed the positive life and impact that Jacqui has made for her family. They, too, have tried to provide better, healthier environments for their families. Jacqui told me that her greatest success is the new pattern she created as the mother of two strong, loving boys and the great relationship they share.

Naysayers may not necessarily mean to harm you. Like the voices in our heads, they are doing their best to keep you safe by not letting you try something new that might lead to failure. Kathryn wanted to become an entrepreneur. She was a single mother with a large mortgage and a steady job. A prominent engineer and scientist, she felt that her heart would sing near the report-writing stage of a project. I had the privilege of collaborating with her on several projects. Our talents meshed perfectly. I'm a visual thinker, so creating figures and tables was my jam. Her passion was writing. We would joke that I'd create the diagrams, and she would write the words around them.

Over the years, Kathryn would lament, "I just want to write. I want to do what I love." However, the corporation that she worked for was not large enough for her to be its full-time technical writer. The only way she could write full time was to create her own business based on her writing skills. This was scary, given her responsibilities as the sole provider for her daughter. And such an endeavor was inherently risky because she might lose their house.

Step by calculated step, Kathryn slowly started to put the pieces in place to start her own business. She also came to realize that her values did not align with those of the corporation she worked for, and it started to drag her down. Between her longing to write and the desire to change directions, it seemed like the perfect window of time to strike out as an entrepreneur. I agreed to be her Battle Buddy and help her in the process.

Everything was going to plan until the day Kathryn went on vacation to visit her parents and was brave enough to tell them she was ready to pull the trigger and execute her plan. It did not go well. She came home deflated. Her parents' risk aversion got the better of them, and they tried to talk her out of it.

"Stay at your current job; it's not that bad," they said. "You have a mortgage and a daughter to take care of."

Her dad told her that he had hated his job for twenty years but stuck with it for the stability of the family. He reminded her that he didn't start his own business until she, her brother, and her sister were all out of college.

"What do you know about entrepreneurship?" her father asked.

"How will you make money?" her mother added.

Her parents' fears placed doubt in her mind that grew by the day. Coupled with a healthy dose of guilt for taking such a risk, Kathryn was left feeling stalled and depressed. We spoke after Kathryn returned from visiting her parents. She told me, "Maybe now is not the right time." The naysayers had won that round. A door opened in her mind, and the Mean Little Voice and Sneaky Little Bastard strode right in.

As her Battle Buddy, I let her have a few days to sort things out. Work was becoming increasingly intolerable, so I asked her to remember her love of writing. Over the phone, I could hear the strain in her voice and her deep yearning to create polished documents that were clear, engaging, audience-focused, and grammatically correct for engineers and scientists, who are notoriously poor writers. She even conceptualized a coaching and education program. We went over her accomplishments and began rebuilding her armor. We closely looked at how much she had done already, and in the process, rebuilt her confidence. Kathryn remembered why she wanted to be a full-time writer and honed her blade. Today, she is thriving with her own company, writing and sharing her knowledge in the hope that others may become better writers as well.

Looking back at Kathryn's situation, I see that in many ways, it is like Jacqui's. There could be jealousy in her parents' statements

Courage isn't about not being afraid. It's about being afraid but doing it anyway.

because her father chose to endure twenty years at a job he did not like instead of starting his business sooner.

For both Jacqui and Kathryn, it took a great deal of courage to stand up for themselves. Whether it's leaning on a Battle Buddy or holding onto a dream so tightly that you need to leave your naysayers behind, you must find your form of courage. It's that little spark powered by your why. Courage isn't about not being afraid. It's about being afraid but doing it anyway.

I AM THE STORM

If you have failed, had a setback, or dealt with a naysayer and need some help working through the issue, there are a few solutions you can try. My colleague Michael found several beneficial ones throughout his life. As a kid with ADHD, he couldn't sit still and was always moving about. He became intrigued by the idea of having a confident mindset in the third grade because he was also petrified to speak up in class. Michael eventually found solace in books. Because he felt like he couldn't talk to anybody about situations in his life, he would read. A bookmobile—basically a Winnebago full of books—would visit his tiny town at regular intervals. But the problem was that there was a limit on how many books you could check out at a time. He would read them so quickly that his mother eventually needed to build a relationship with the bookmobile owner so that Michael could check out more than the standard allotment.

Coming into adulthood, Michael realized that he didn't have time to read all the books he wanted. As someone who was best at verbally processing the information roaming around in his head but who had trouble talking about his problems to others, he decided to start talking to the page. He just started writing, or more specifically, journaling. Sometimes it was just ten minutes a day; sometimes it was longer. After reading Ethan Kross's book *Chatter,* he started using the method called "distanced self-talk." Kross explains how using your name when talking to yourself can help create psychological distance, which can reduce stress and improve decision-making. For example, instead of asking himself, "Why am I upset?" he would ask, "Why is Michael upset about this?" In this way, he feels more confident about advising himself. He conceived three questions that he would answer when he had a failure or a setback, or was just in a general funk:

1. Why is Michael upset about this?
2. What is Michael going to do about this?
3. Why hasn't Michael already done it?

As he began to create the answers to these questions, his head started to clear.

Sitting down and journaling can help get the angst out of our heads so we can start sorting through all our issues. Michael recommends that those who have not journaled ask themselves if they like having conversations with people about what is bothering them. If the answer is yes, keep doing that. Journaling might not be for you. If the answer is no or there are insecurities and thoughts that they would rather not reveal but still want to work out, journaling might be a solution.

Luckily for the journalers, there are different means to express your thoughts in a manner to be preserved. There's the traditional way of writing things on a piece of paper. It can be done via electronic means through computers, tablets, or phones. Michael started using Google Docs as his preferred form of getting his thoughts out. Most impressively, when he opened his document recently, he received a warning signal that his Google Doc had reached the allowable character limit. Who knew Google Docs had a limit? We looked it up. It's 1,020,000 characters, or about 400,000 words.

Michael also recommends that if you just need to talk it out, several phone apps can dictate for you. When he doesn't feel like typing, he just jumps in his car and takes a drive. He'll first grab an iced tea and a breakfast sandwich, and as soon as he finishes eating, he verbally journals into his phone, and his phone types it out.

Michael's initial quest for a confident mindset has helped him find the courage to speak up, which has morphed as he has matured. He now looks internally to understand why he behaves in certain ways to conflict or adverse situations, why others behave the way they do, why he might be struggling with this or that, and why some efforts are easier or harder than they should be. He also uses journaling to keep at bay the Mean Little Voice that is always trying to convince him he is not good enough.

Journaling is a tricky thing and requires consistency. Many studies have been performed on its positive outcomes. If you are interested in trying this method, pick a time each day, set an alarm for ten minutes, and just write what is on your mind. Do this for two weeks straight, with no breaks. At the end of the two weeks, make your own assessment of whether it has helped sort out some of the issues that might be plaguing you. Again, journaling isn't for everyone, but it has helped so many that it cannot be discounted.

For me, I've taken a different path. As I am a public speaker, rejections are part of the process. You lose a speaking engagement to another speaker, they are looking for a different topic, or it's just not the right fit. I've never been able to take rejection well; it always feels personal. I know I should be better at it. Maybe I'm too sensitive, or I'm just human. I'm working to adjust my thinking process and use it as a learning experience. But I'll be open with you; there are days when I put my head on the desk and wonder, *Can I really do this? Is this sustainable? Do I have what it takes? Is this too hard?*

In those moments, I think about my accomplishments and my why. My current goal is to be a great public speaker, and my why is that I have a passionate message and mission to help as many people as possible.

When I am having those days when I feel lost in the labyrinth, worrying about financial security or my prospects drying up, I recite my new mantra. Yes, I have a new mantra. There is a common saying in the military: "Fate says to the Warrior, 'You cannot weather the storm.' The Warrior whispers back, 'I am the storm.'" I imagine the storm clouds on the horizon, black, billowing, and threatening.

With my head in my palms, I remember my message, my mission, and my mantra. "I am a warrior." And I repeat, "I am the storm." I am that force of nature, the one that is wild, terrifying, and cannot be contained. I am the one who will overcome my worries and the petty obstacles that are in my way. I say this when it feels like hope is dying. If we are still considering weapons for our Warriors, my mantra is the dagger at my side, there for when I need more than just the sword.

In chapter 1, I spoke about the craft store's motivational wooden block signs and their bland affirmations. Now that you have done the deep work of understanding your value and worth, that deep-down, intense desire to create something new, you are ready for your mantra. My mantra might not be the one for you. For me, it works. Find one that resonates with who you know you are and want to become.

The craft store didn't have an "I am the storm" mantra block, so I went on Etsy and found one. It sits just to the right of my desk. On those days when I feel lost or I've had a major setback or even a failure, I look at that block and know that I have a storm inside ready to get out.

WARRIOR EXERCISE

Think about what your mantra will be when you need it the most.

WARRIOR DEBRIEF

1. Failure is a common part of any journey; it's what you do after that counts. Setbacks can be opportunities to reassess and pivot rather than reasons to quit.
2. Naysayers are often those closest to us who may unintentionally or intentionally discourage us from pursuing our goals. When dealing with naysayers, lean on your Battle Buddies and maintain your strong sense of purpose.
3. Journaling and repeating your mantras can help you to stay focused and motivated.

8

LEARNING TO LIVE WITH AND EVEN EMBRACE THE VOICES

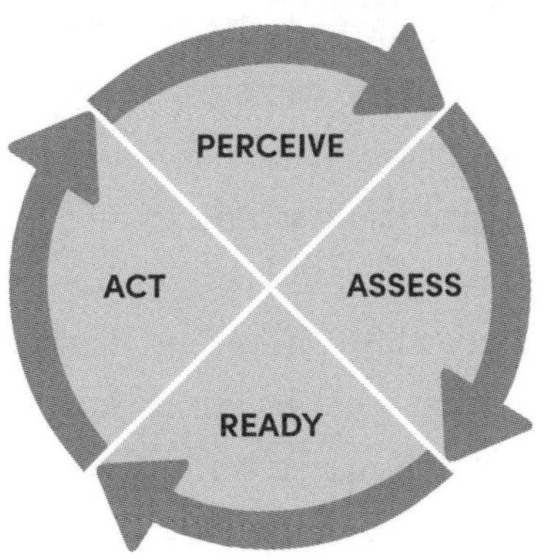

I initially met Scott during my deployment to Iraq in 2008. He was assigned to the outpost Camp Korean Village to provide operational support for the US Marine Corps's light-armored reconnaissance vehicles. When the time came to relieve one of the convoy commanders of duty due to a lack of leadership ability, we looked at Scott to fill that role. He was a convoy commander during his 2004–2005 tour and would be a perfect fit. We knew that with his prior experience, calm demeanor, and solid leadership skills, he would be perfect.

Being on the convoy teams was probably the scariest job of the battalion. I was the operations officer, which meant that I was in charge of—you guessed it—all battalion operations, including construction projects, reconnaissance missions for infrastructure, and our three convoy teams. Because our convoys traveled at night, it was the perfect time for insurgents to hide roadside bombs and pressure-triggered explosive devices in the road. Our convoys would detect or hit one about every three days. For whatever reason, this always happened at 2:00 a.m. The watch officer would then send someone to wake me up, and I'd head to our command operations center to lead the response. Because this happened so frequently, I soon developed strong relationships with my convoy commanders. Scott was always the calmest on the radio as we talked through the situation: whether anyone was injured, the state of the vehicles, or whether there was any additional enemy activity.

Since Iraq, we have maintained ties. I have watched him get promoted and take on additional responsibilities. Now that both of us are retired, we can have more cordial conversations and no longer need to call each other by our ranks and titles.

When I began doing research for this book, Scott was one of the people I reached out to. I knew how calm he was under pressure and wondered if he ever had the little voices challenge his decision-making process. I thought someone so grounded and levelheaded might not even know what I was talking about.

His answer: "Oh, heck yes!"

He told me that he had a bit of a rough upbringing, including a grandmother who knew the Mafia in Las Vegas before it was cool. Scott's tendency, once he sees a challenge, is to just go for it. He talks himself into a fight before the fight even happens. There is no chance for the Cousins to sneak in first. His mind also prepares for the negative outcomes and how to resolve them before they come into play. Scott's cycle through the Warrior Framework allows him to Perceive, Assess, and Ready so quickly that Act is the first logical step.

As we continued to talk about different subjects, I brought up celebrating his wins. Scott told me, "When I start recognizing my small wins, that's when the battle really begins for me."

Wait, what? After all that he had been through, including multiple overseas combat tours, something as simple as recognizing his small wins would trigger the Warrior Framework?

He told me that when he starts to recognize his wins, his Warrior voice starts to prepare to hear his Cousins, which he named Frank (the Mean Little Voice) and Gertrude (the Sneaky Little Bastard). Applying concepts from *The Art of War*, he told me that he knows himself well and wants to be ready for the fight. It will happen, and it's easier to defeat the enemy you know before they have time to prepare.

Many of us may feel at war with the voices in our heads. But as Sun Tzu says, "If you know the enemy and know yourself, you need not fear the result of a hundred battles." Through this book, I hope that you have achieved a better sense of yourself and all that you are capable of by documenting your daily wins, acknowledging your accomplishments, and internalizing your strengths. I hope that

It's easier to defeat the enemy you know before they have time to prepare.

you also have a better understanding of who the "enemy" may be. Whether it's the Mean Little Voice who actively tries to tear you down and discourage you, or the Sneaky Little Bastard who tries to delay or steer you in a different direction, you now have the ability to Perceive their existence and Assess whether they are truly looking to hold you back. Your Warrior stands Ready to help defeat them as you prepare to Act on your well-prepared plan.

I can't tell you that the voices will ever go away. Especially if you continue to push yourself to grow and continually try new things. But as you practice moving through the Warrior Framework, it will get easier, and they will get quieter.

TAKING IT UP A NOTCH

Kris never went to college. Instead, he spent his college years touring with a band and providing their music production. He found his niche in the love of technology.

After he left the band, Kris went to work for a large health-care company. But the day-in-and-day-out grind soon began to wear on him. He was completely dissatisfied with where he was, but the idea of having to update his résumé and go on interviews, well, it was just *ugghh* and not something he wanted to do.

The alternative was to go out on his own. But the thought of the risk and having to deal with personnel, insurance, taxes, and regulations seemed too much. After all, Kris knew nothing about running a business.

One morning he woke up, and something had changed. He couldn't put a finger on it, but he knew, deep in his soul, what he had to do. He had to go out on his own and start a consultancy. He bought a stack of books covering finance, marketing, sales, contracts, and project management and ravenously consumed the information. In 2007, he opened his first business.

Naturally talented in electronics and technology, he has become a serial entrepreneur, creating multiple successful small businesses. Yet, the Mean Little Voice was always whispering in his ear, *You aren't really an entrepreneur; you never went to college.* He had a persistent fear that at any moment, disaster was going to strike. He was afraid that he would say something wrong, or somebody with an MBA would mention a topic that he knew nothing about. When he entered a room with other successful entrepreneurs, he honestly believed that he wasn't worthy enough to be there. He thought that they looked at him like he was a lucky fluke, and he felt like a fraud.

He turned to a business coach, who asked if he had ever heard of impostor syndrome. When he heard this, all he could say was, "Oh my goodness." Immediately, a weight was lifted off his shoulders. These feelings he experienced had a scientific name and were being studied by psychologists. An incredible amount of the population experiences these same feelings. He was not alone!

Kris mentally started sifting through the ideas and realized that they were made up in his head. He named his Mean Little Voice "The Impostor." Once he could identify The Impostor, he was able to start to separate the truth from the lies.

When he started talking to colleagues about it, they would respond the same way. "Oh, my gosh, I thought that was just me!" The continual realizations and aha moments from those he spoke with motivated him to dig deeper into the subject. He came up with three realizations:

1. Those who are content have no real impostor syndrome. They aren't growing or trying to better themselves.
2. Real impostors don't have impostor syndrome.

They know they are faking it and have no actual fears of being called out as frauds.

3. The more ambitious you are, the more boundaries you push, and the more you find yourself in over your head, the more you start to feel like a fraud.

In his life, Kris began the cycle of the Warrior Framework: Perceive, Assess, Ready, and Act. He has become extremely aware of The Impostor when the voice creeps in, telling him, *Oh, you're at risk* or *You're going to embarrass yourself.* He has been able to develop the tools to respond to it, shut it down, and counteract it quickly—so much so that The Impostor doesn't affect him or slow him down very much.

But Kris went a step further. As he was cataloging all the times he heard the voices, he made the startling realization that it was during times of growth. Now when he hears the voice, he gets a little excited and giddy. "Oh, there's a possibility here. I might be on to something great."

I realize this might feel like next-level stuff, but you are at the point in the process where you should no longer resent the Mean Little Voice and the Sneaky Little Bastard. You have the tools and the framework to quickly separate their messages from basic instincts and intuition and can assess whether they are rational or not. You know your strengths and can shut the Cousins down.

WARRIOR EXERCISE

What has happened when you hear the Cousins and move forward anyway?

____

____

____

Like Kris, you may find that when you start to hear the Cousins, it may mean that you are on the brink of something great. You may also begin to get excited and giddy.

I want you to also recognize that in this moment, right now, you are in a remarkable position. You are stretching, growing, and working outside your comfort zone. You have never done what you have been planning to do, which means you are already in a new place in your life. That's exciting! Embrace your new setting and keep going. The only direction to go is toward the attainment of your goal. With continued practice, you can look at new and upcoming obstacles and not flinch. You are ready to move forward with confidence, stare adversity in the eye, and say, "Not today."

WARRIOR DEBRIEF

1. You now have the tools through the Warrior Framework to move forward with confidence—you Perceive the voices in your stream of consciousness; Assess whether they are friend or foe; Ready your Warrior through discipline, resilience, training, and preparedness; and then Act.
2. You may even learn to embrace the excitement and growth that comes with hearing the voices.
3. Continue to move forward with confidence, even in the face of adversity, and view challenges as opportunities for personal and professional development.

9

GO FORTH AND DO GREAT THINGS

For about one-third of my childhood, it was just me and my mom. She wanted to make sure I was a well-rounded kid, so she signed me up for swimming, soccer, ballet, softball, and track. And she was always in the stands cheering me on.

Three weeks after graduating college, I shipped off to Pensacola, Florida, for OCS and the infamous GunnerySergeantWoollettUnitedStatesMarineCorps. I had always loved long-distance running, and let me tell you, he made sure we did a lot of it. The week before I was commissioned, we had our final physical fitness test, which included a mile-and-a-half run. Miraculously, I completed it with a time of 10:02, which for me is pretty good. I'd still rather run ten miles at an easy pace than feel like I need to sprint for the entire mile and a half.

I had some time off between OCS in sunny Florida and Civil

Engineer Corps Officer School in foggy Port Hueneme, California. I hopped on the I-10 and headed west in my Toyota Corolla, detouring north in New Mexico to the small town of Ruidoso, where my mom and new stepdad had a cabin in the mountains. Nestled at an elevation of seven thousand feet, it was a drastic change from sea level. I needed to stay in shape, so each morning I laced up my sneakers, and despite the chilly mountain temperatures, I would opt for a T-shirt and shorts. My lungs protested loudly at the thin, crisp air, yet I still ran, taking in the towering pine trees, the little brook by the road, and the quaint cabins tucked in on either side.

One morning I asked my mom, "Do you want to run with me?"

I think I shocked her.

"You run too far," she started to protest. "And you run too fast." Then she added, "I've never run before."

Now I was shocked.

I realized that throughout my childhood, she never had time for her own hobbies. She worked long hours so she could take care of me. Weekends were typically spent concentrating on me, making sure to get me to practice or rehearsals on time. And she was always in the stands, cheering me on. It was always about me, never about her.

Well, this would not do. I convinced her that we would go for a walk with little jogs interspersed. It would be a fun mother-daughter adventure and time for us to catch up since I had been gone for several months.

It was surprisingly damp that morning. The dew sat heavy on the ferns and underbrush. No birds chirped or sang. The only sound was the gurgle of the brook by the road. My mom, clad in sweatpants, a sweatshirt, gloves, and a hat, was ready. Out we went into the mist at a nice leisurely pace.

As we strolled down the road toward town, I suggested, "Let's just run to that power pole." We picked up the pace and jogged for about twenty-five yards, slowing back down to a walk. After a five-minute breather, I said, "Let's just jog to the stop sign."

Signs, poles, bridges, driveways, and lawn art all made targets to jog for twenty-five to thirty yards at a time. Each morning, we'd get up, gear up, and go out for our morning walk-jog. It was fun, and my mom was soon picking the targets, each one a little farther away.

After a week, I said my goodbyes and continued my journey to California. But for my mom, her running journey was just getting started. Each day, she would set her targets, and she told me it was my voice in her head that would say, "Let's just jog to the intersection."

It turns out she kind of liked running. This was something she could do for herself. She heard that the Ruidoso Parks and Recreation Department was hosting a 5K fun run. Given the option of walking or jogging, she chose to walk it since she had not been training. She found a friend, and off they went. Part of the way into the race, she decided, "Well, I think I'll try to jog a little bit." Little did she know that the Ruidoso Parks and Rec Department had jogging police.

"Ma'am, are you a walker?"

"Yes," she shyly answered.

"Then you need to stop jogging" was the man's curt reply.

Apparently they were strict about this kind of thing. She held herself back, but she knew that based on her experiences up and down the road from the cabin, she could run it. At the end of the race, they announced, "Runners, next month is the Alamogordo 10K. Sign up now for a discount."

She asked the person next to her, "How far is 10K?"

They simply replied, "It's about six miles."

She thought, *Oh, there's no way! Who runs six miles? Nobody runs six miles.*

But the possibility, the thought that she *could* do it, overrode the Sneaky Little Bastard. "Well, I think I'll do it."

Although she hadn't been training, she walked and jogged the 10K the next month and earned her first running medal. She told me, "I think I just got it because I was a participant, but that was pretty neat."

Mom joined the West Texas Running Club, got the right shoes, and over the next several months, trained and traveled to races throughout eastern New Mexico and west and north Texas. This was also when she started reading *Runner's World* magazine. In the back was an article about where to run your first marathon. The author recommended the one at Walt Disney World because you could take your time, enjoy it, and make it memorable.

That's when her Sneaky Little Bastard started to speak up. *Who am I to do something like that? I'm not going to run a marathon. Not everyone can do it. Only 1 percent of the world's population has ever run a marathon. Let's try something easier.*

She started to think through all the 5K and 10K races she had been in so far. Sure, they had been hard, and she wasn't the fastest runner out there. But she had finished each one, even medaling in some events with advantageous age brackets. She had run in one of the highest sanctioned 10Ks in the world, at eighty-six hundred feet in Cloudcroft, New Mexico. She had run on vacation in Finland on a gorgeous fall day with cool, crisp orange leaves falling around her. She had run in races in honor of her aunt for Alzheimer's disease and her sister for breast cancer.

Yet she told no one of the desire to run a marathon. That dream was too big. Who would believe her and support this crazy endeavor? She trained in silence, waking up at 5:30 a.m. to run around the local community college, working up the courage to finally tell the family, "I'm running a marathon."

What she didn't expect was an outpouring of support from the whole family. Siblings, nephews, nieces, and I all rallied behind her. This was our moment to be in the stands, cheering her on.

The Disney World Marathon held in January 2002 was the coldest one on record. Somewhat bundled up against the freezing temperatures, she started running. It was cold.

And then it started raining.

Then it started sleeting.

Thirteen miles into the race, she neared a turnoff point. Half-marathoners turned left and completed their race. Marathoners went straight. And that left looked soooo inviting. *You are too wet and cold. This is far enough. We could finish sooner and get warm. We can always run a marathon later.*

Looking down at herself, she saw she was soaking wet. Her shoes were heavy from all the rainwater they absorbed and squished with each step. Then she recalled her previous victories and the months of training that had gone into being here on this particular day.

"Well, I'm wet. I'm already here. I'll just keep going. Let's just jog to the next signpost."

Step by literal step, picking her targets, taking pictures with a soaked Minnie and Mickey, enjoying the sodden bands and drenched cheer squads that lined the route, she finished.

Since she started running at the age of forty-seven, she has completed four marathons, six half-marathons, and over twenty 5K and 10K races. She finalized her running career with a half-marathon the day after her seventieth birthday at Disneyland Paris and the accompanying half-marathon a month later back where it all began at Disney World. She told me, "I guess I wanted to prove to myself I could do something, something that not very many people on this earth do."

When she started running, her only goal was to make it to the next target. Never would she have believed what was possible.

You probably think this chapter is about taking things one signpost at a time. It's true that you can do impossible things that way. But I think you already know that. You finished this book, one exercise and one chapter at a time. But I tell you this story about my mom and running, not because I want you to put yourself in my mom's shoes, but because I want you to put yourself in mine. I want you to take all you've learned in this book, all you understand, and not just make what you want possible, but do the same for others. I want you to be the person who says, "Hey, Mom, do you want to go for a run?"

YOUR NEW RESPONSIBILITY

I believe I was put on this planet to help as many people as possible, to lead and guide them to become their best selves. And now, in turn, you must do the same. You have learned to recognize and overcome the insecurities and doubts in you. Now it's time to turn your perception outward.

We are constantly thinking, whether it's bad or good stuff, about ourselves. But in the end, it's still all about ourselves. Look at the simple understanding that you now have. Look at this simple pathway and framework that you can now employ. Realize what you know how to do. Your dreams are not just possible. They're probable because of what you learned in this book. This book is not just for your current goal. It can be used for smaller goals, future goals, and better yet, those goals from your past that you previously gave up on. So what are you going to do now?

What if you could help other people so their dreams become probable? Can you take this knowledge and help others? Can you help your kids? Your neighbor? Someone in your church? Or someone in the cubicle next to you?

We all have friends, family, and colleagues who have the Cousins running rampant in their heads. Maybe they are uncomfortable stepping into a room where they might look different, are a different gender or age, or have a dissimilar philosophy to yours. They may feel like an "only." You may also start to notice coworkers who enter a meeting and stay quiet, not voicing their opinions because you can see they don't feel confident or that they belong. If up to 82 percent of the world has had impostor syndrome and fears of failure or success, that means four out of your five colleagues, loved ones, or friends are susceptible. You will see it in their eyes—the self-doubt, the longing, or the need for a change in their status quo. They, too, have Warriors waiting to wake up.

The greatest thing you could do now is to *own* what you have learned from this book. Do you want to be the master of it? Go out, teach it, and help others imagine what their worlds could look like. Those who teach others are 90 percent more likely to reinforce their own understanding in a deeper and more meaningful way.

> **Imagine the difference you can make and what the world could look like.**

Find, help, and guide them so they can be the best they can be. So they are not afraid. So they stop pretending to be someone else or finally feel worthy of achieving their best. So, like you, they are ready to reach for greatness and dare to rise to be their best.

Imagine the difference you can make and what the world could look like.

Each of us is capable of wonderful things. I beg of you to not be one of those people who, on their deathbeds, are looking back at their lives and saying, “I wish I would have.” I can think of no greater regret than to pass up an opportunity. H. Jackson Brown Jr. summed up this sentiment well: “Twenty years from now you will be more disappointed by the things that you didn’t do than by the ones you did do. So, sail away from the safe harbor. Explore, dream, and discover.”

Share. Teach. Make a difference.

My Warriors, go do great things.

BIBLIOGRAPHY

Achor, Shawn. *Big Potential: How Transforming the Pursuit of Success Raises Our Achievement, Happiness, and Well-Being*. Currency, 2018.

Amabile, Teresa M., and Steven J. Kramer. "The Power of Small Wins." *Harvard Business Review*. May 2011. https://hbr.org/2011/05/the-power-of-small-wins.

Bravata, Dena M., Divya K. Madhusudhan, Michael Boroff, and Kevin O. Cokley. "Prevalence, Predictors, and Treatment of Impostor Syndrome: A Systematic Review." *Journal of Mental Health and Clinical Psychology* 4, no. 3 (2020): 12–16.

Brown, H. Jackson Jr. *P.S. I Love You*. Rutledge Hill Press, 1990.

Clance, Pauline Rose, and Suzanne A. Imes. "The Impostor Phenomenon in High Achieving Women: Dynamics and Therapeutic Intervention." *Psychotherapy: Theory, Research & Practice* 15, no. 3 (1978): 241–247.

Cowan, Emily T., Yiwen Zhang, Benjamin M. Rottman, and Vishnu P. Murty. "The Effects of Mnemonic Variability and Spacing on Memory over Multiple Timescales." *Proceedings of the National Academy of Sciences of the United States of America* 121, no. 12 (2024): e2311077121. https://doi.org/10.1073/pnas.2311077121.

Dweck, Carol S. *Mindset: The New Psychology of Success*. Random House, 2006.

Eagleson, Claire, Sarra Hayes, Andrew Matthews, Gemma Perman, and Colette R. Hirsch. "The Power of Positive Thinking: Pathological

Worry Is Reduced by Thought Replacement in Generalized Anxiety Disorder." *Behaviour Research and Therapy* 78 (2016): 13–18. http://doi.org/10.1016/j.brat.2015.12.017.

Edelman, Marian Wright. "A Conversation with Marian Wright Edelman." *Mother Jones* (May–June 1991).

Fuller, Thomas. *Gnomologia: Adagies and Proverbs; Wise Sentences and Witty Sayings*. B. Barker, 1732.

Health Reporter. January 3, 2024. "110+ Running Statistics and Facts in 2024." https://healthreporter.com/news/running-statistics/.

Hume, David. "The Natural History of Religion." In *Essays and Treatises on Several Subjects,* vol. 2. A. Millar, 1757.

Indegene. "Understanding the Science Behind Learning Retention." https://www.indegene.com/what-we-think/reports/understanding-science-behind-learning-retention

Kelso, Kris. *Overcoming the Impostor: Silence Your Inner Critic and Lead with Confidence*. Dexterity, 2021.

Koyenikan, Idowu. *Wealth for All: Living a Life of Success at the Edge of Your Ability,* 1st ed. International Publications, 2014.

Kross, Ethan. *Chatter: The Voice in Our Head, Why It Matters, and How to Harness It*. Crown, 2021.

Linkagoal. "Research Reveals Fear of Failure Has Us All Shaking in Our Boots This Halloween." *GlobeNewswire*. October 14, 2015. https://www.globenewswire.com/news-release/2015/10/14/1060928/0/en/Research-Reveals-Fear-of-Failure-Has-Us-All-Shaking-in-Our-Boots-This-Halloween.html.

Marder, Ben, Ana Javornik, Kang Qi, John Oliver, Laura Lavertu, and Kirsten Cowan. "Does LinkedIn Cause Imposter Syndrome? An Empirical Examination of Well-Being and Consumption-Related Effects." *Psychology & Marketing* 41, no. 3 (2024): 492–511. https://doi.org/10.1002/mar.21926.

Matthews, Gail. "The Impact of Writing Goals on Goal Attainment: An Eight-Month Study." *International Journal of Behavioral Science* 2, no. 1 (2007): 69–79.

Matthews, Gail. "Study Confirms Smart Strategies for Achieving Goals." *Dominican University of California*. 2015. https://www.dominican.edu/sites/default/files/2020-02/gailmatthews-harvard-goals-researchsummary.pdf.

McTiernan, John, director. *The Hunt for Red October*. Los Angeles: Paramount Pictures, 1990. 2 hr., 15 min. DVD.

Merzenich, Michael. *Soft-Wired: How the New Science of Brain Plasticity Can Change Your Life*. Parnassus Publishing, 2013.

Norwest Venture Partners. "Findings from Our CEO Journey Study." *Norwest Venture Partners Blog*. August 22, 2018. https://www.nvp.com/blog/insights-norwests-2018-ceo-journey-study/.

Orwell, George. *Why I Write*. Penguin Books, 2014.

Paul Ekman Group. "The Science of 'Inside Out.'" *Paul Ekman Group Blog*. July 3, 2015. https://www.paulekman.com/blog/the-science-of-inside-out/.

Sakai, Kuniyoshi L., Keita Umejima, Takuya Ibaraki, and Takahiro Yamazaki. "Paper Notebooks vs. Mobile Devices: Brain Activation Differences During Memory Retrieval." *Frontiers in Behavioral Neuroscience* (2021). https://doi.org/10.3389/fnbeh.2021.634158.

Schad, Tom. "U.S. Gymnastics' Brody Malonc Misses Out on Olympic All-Around Final in a Big Surprise." *USA Today*. July 27, 2024. https://www.usatoday.com/story/sports/olympics/2024/07/27/us-mens-gymnastics-olympics-qualifying-results/74569291007/.

Tandon, Mahek. "100 Gym Membership + Retention Statistics You Need to Know in 2025." Smart Health Clubs. February 22, 2025. https://smarthealthclubs.com/blog/100-gym-membership-retention-statistics/.

Tzu, Sun. *The Art of War*, trans. Lionel Giles. Luzac & Co.

Walter, Chip. *Last Ape Standing: The Seven-Million-Year Story of How and Why We Survived*. Bloomsbury, 2013.

ACKNOWLEDGMENTS

To my incredible ski buddy, hiking companion, and partner in crime, Sean. You inspire me and push me to be my best. Without your unconditional support, this book would never have come to life. I love you!

To the greatest mom on the planet, Janie Phillips. It all started with you, quite literally. You have been the greatest supporter and cheerleader anyone could ever hope for. But more importantly, you are so incredibly strong and the rock that I can always count on.

A big thanks to all the wonderful friends, colleagues, and clients who permitted me to interview them for this book, including: Lt. Col. Tammy Barlette, Dr. Glenn Canares, Paul Costanzo, Michelle "Mace" Curran, Phil Gerbyshak, Katie Francis, Michael Hudson, Kris Kelso, Anna Nelson, CDR Don Petersen, Greg Pfeiffer, Jacqui Pfeiffer, Thomas Qualman, and Master Chief Scott Shaner. I also want to give a shout-out to my Battle Buddy, Doug Whimpey. Thank you for always being there for me, through the rough times and the fun ones.

As this book came to life, I enlisted the help of some spectacular test readers. These poor souls read the rough manuscript chapter by chapter and provided invaluable feedback that made the final product so much better. Thank you to Susan Barber,

Michael Bennett, Tucker Blythe, Angela Chason, Wendy Key, Jacqui Pfeiffer, Justine Ramdas, Scott Shaner, and Amber Sigler. I truly appreciate your contributions.

Writing a book is never a solo job. I received so much professional guidance, support, encouragement, and compassion from AJ Harper, Laura Stone, Sade Amherd, and all the wonderful litterateurs of the Top Three Books Author Community. Each day I looked forward to our writing sprints.

Getting this book into your hands would not have been possible without the launch and publication teams. Barbara Caraballo, you kept all the trains running on time. Thank you for your encouragement and motivation throughout the entire process. To Emily Harper, your endless positivity and creativity has always made you, Maggie Dunlap, and your entire team so much fun to work with. I'm looking forward to all the future work we will do together. To the amazing team at Amplify Publishing Group. Naren Aryal, thank you for believing in me and this book. Jenna Scafuri, thank you for guiding the process and to help get this book into the world. I would be remiss if I did not also thank my good friend, Josh Bernoff, who believed in me so much that he introduced me to Naren. A huge thanks to the Brand Builders Group and Taylor Spradling; you are such a shot of energy. I learned so much from you, but also more about myself, through your guidance.

And finally, to my office manager, Pliny, you were always there to keep me company and increase morale. Your timely and unremitting need to sit on my keyboard, notes, and storyboard provided a much-needed work-life balance. And to my two interns, Fenris and Freya, thank you for allowing me to take you on walks through the woods so I could unravel my thoughts and open up to creative ideas.

ABOUT THE AUTHOR

Jenn Donahue is an international keynote speaker, retired US Navy captain, business coach, and one of America's leading experts on leadership and personal growth.

With a PhD in engineering, in her spare time she works on large-scale, high-profile geotechnical earthquake engineering projects. She is the founder and owner of JL Donahue Engineering and Dare to Rise. She also lectures at UC Berkeley, UCLA, Cal Poly, and Virginia Tech.

Over her twenty-seven-year military career, Jenn has built a bridge across the Euphrates River in the midst of the Iraq War, commanded an eight-hundred-personnel battalion in Afghanistan, and constructed combat outposts in the middle of deserts filled with insurgents.